It's another Quality Book from CGP

This Workbook has been designed to accompany our GCSE Revision Guide. It'll test you on everything you need to know for GCSE ICT.

It's also got the odd daft bit in to try and make the whole thing at least vaguely entertaining for you.

What CGP is all about

Our sole aim here at CGP is to produce the highest quality books — carefully written, immaculately presented and dangerously close to being funny.

Then we work our socks off to get them out to you — at the cheapest possible prices.

Contents

Section One — What is a Computer?

Data and Computer Systems ... 1
Computer Systems ... 2
Types of Computer ... 3
Networks — LANs and WANs ... 4
Networks — Different Configurations ... 5
Network Security ... 6

Section Two — Parts of a Computer System

Input Devices ... 7
The CPU ... 10
Output Devices — Printers ... 11
Output Devices — More Printers ... 12
Other Kinds of Output Device ... 13
Data Storage — ROM and RAM ... 15
Data Storage — Backing Storage ... 16
Operating Systems — Main Tasks ... 18
Operating Systems — User Interfaces ... 19

Section Three — Using a Computer System

Data Capture ... 20
Data Validation and Verification ... 21
Data Storage ... 22
Data Processing ... 23
Accessing and Updating Data ... 24
Data Presentation ... 25

Section Four — Systems Analysis

Step One — Identify the Problem ... 26
Analysis — The Feasibility Study ... 27
Design — Input, Process, Output ... 28
Design — Top-Down and Data-Flow ... 29
Design — System Flowcharts ... 30
Testing and User Documentation ... 31
Implementation and Evaluation ... 32

Section Five — Text and Image Processing Software

Word Processing Basics ... 33
Text Formatting and Editing ... 34
Improving Presentation ... 35
Word Processing — Advanced Features ... 36
Graphics — Creating Images ... 38
Graphics — Manipulating Vector Images ... 39
Graphics — Manipulating Bitmap Images ... 40
Graphics — Computer-Aided Design ... 42
Desktop Publishing — Basics ... 43
DTP and Other Presentation Software ... 44

Section Six — Spreadsheets and Databases

Spreadsheets — The Basics 45
Spreadsheets — Creating and Improving 46
Spreadsheets — Simple Formulas 47
Spreadsheets — The Trickier Stuff 48
Spreadsheets — Graphs and Charts 49
Databases — Creating One 50
Databases — Sorts and Queries 51
Databases — Reports 52

Section Seven — Measurement, Control and Simulation

Measurement — Data Logging 53
Logging Period and Logging Interval 54
Control — Basic Systems 55
Control Systems — Two Examples 56
Process Control and Control Language 57
Modelling and Simulation — Basic Stuff 58
Spreadsheet Models and Simulations 59
Simulations — Flight Simulators 60

Section Eight — The Internet

Internet Basics 61
E-mail 62
Using the World Wide Web — Navigating 63
Navigating and Downloading 64
Web Page Design 65
Using the Internet — Data Security 66
User-Generated Content 67
Social Networking 69
Online Audio and Video 71
Online Software 72

Section Nine — Computers in the Real World

Computers in Shops 73
Computers in Banks 74
The Electronic Office 75
Computers in Schools 76
Cars and Traffic Management Systems 77
Computers in the Home 78
Computer Applications — Other Stuff 79

Section Ten — Computers and Society

Computers and the Law 80
Computers and the Workplace 81
Computer Use — Health and Safety Issues 82
Social, Moral and Ethical Issues 83

Published by Coordination Group Publications Ltd.

Contributors:
Roy Chisem
Niall Clarke
Charley Darbishire
Dominic Hall
Thomas Harte
Simon Little
Rob MacDonald
Katherine Reed
Chrissy Williams

With thanks to Neil Burrell for the proofreading.

ISBN: 978 1 84762 173 3

Groovy website: www.cgpbooks.co.uk

Jolly bits of clipart from CorelDRAW®

Printed by Elanders Hindson Ltd, Newcastle upon Tyne.

Data and Computer Systems

Q1 Define the following:

a) Byte
b) ASCII code
c) DVD-ROM capacity
d) Data
e) "Garbage in garbage out" theory

Q2 Copy and complete the table below about data storage:

Name of data type	Approximate size in bytes	Abbreviation
Byte		-
	1000	KB
Megabyte		
	1000 000 000	

Q3 A computerised system has benefits over a paper-based system. One is that a computerised system takes up a lot less space — there's no need for filing cabinets. For each of the statements below, say whether or not they are a benefit of a computerised system.

a) Reports can be generated very quickly.
b) Computerised systems are 100% reliable — they can never fail.
c) There's no need for electricity.
d) More than one person at a time can access the same data from their network PC.
e) Searching for records is very quick.
f) There's no need for loads of time-consuming and expensive training, because computerised systems are always very simple to use.

Q4 Lots of companies have switched from paper-based systems to computerised systems. Briefly describe **six** problems of a paper-based system.

Q5 Copy the sentences below about the problems of computerised systems. Use the words on the enormous gut to fill in the gaps.

a) Setting up a computer system is very .... Big systems in large organisations like the NHS can cost ...... of pounds.
b) Computer systems need people to ...... and use them. ...... costs can be high, and the money is ...... if the person leaves.
c) Computer systems are not perfect — if there's a system ...... or a ...... , then important data might get ....
d) It can be easy to copy ...... and so remove confidential ...... from the system. The system needs to be kept secure from unauthorised users and ....

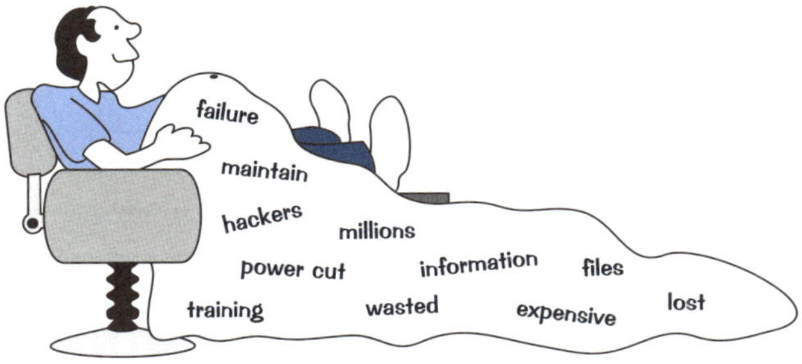

Computer Systems

Q1 Copy the sentence below and fill in the gaps using words in the cloud on the right.

> *A .... is an integrated .... of hardware and .... that enables .... to be input, then .... and the results communicated to the ....*

software
data *processed*
computer system *user*
system

Q2 Put these three sentences in the correct order:

A The results are shown at the output stage.
B Data is entered at the input stage.
C The computer then processes the data.

Q3 *Information needs to be converted into data before it is entered into a computer. This might mean converting the information into a code.*

a) Copy and complete this table of dates and codes.

Date	Code 1	Code 2
6th November 1973	061173	11061973
7th September 1977		
26th December 1908		
26th January 1988		
1st July 1947		
1st July 1946		
24th May 2002		

b) Suggest a problem that might occur with code 1, but not with code 2.

Q4 Copy and complete this diagram, using words from this rat here:

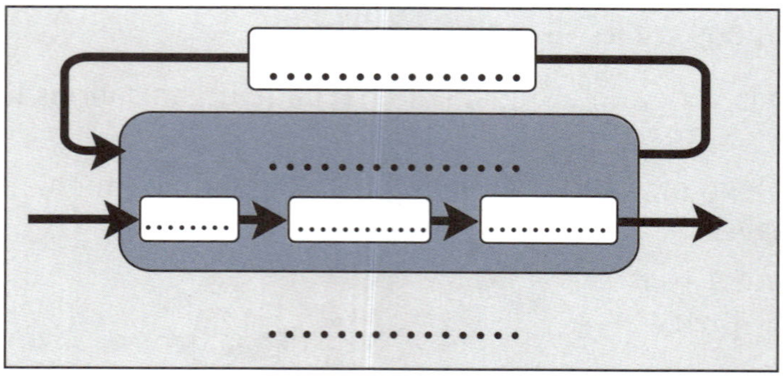

I've got a computer cistern — for more efficient flushing...

There are loads of different ways to encode loads of different things. For example, Microsoft Excel stores all dates as the number of days from January 1st 1900. So today is 37847. Or maybe not.

Types of Computer

Q1 Complete these sentences about the ways people used to classify computers by using the phrases on the right.

a)	Mainframes are...	i)	...in the middle.
b)	Microcomputers are...	ii)	...the biggest.
c)	Minicomputers are...	iii)	...the most common type of computer.

Q2 In which decade were mainframes first developed?

Q3 Explain how servers are different from normal PCs in terms of hardware used and their function.

Q4 Suggest two situations where a mainframe would be a better choice than a group of servers.

Q5 What's the most common type of computer in use today?

Q6 Link each requirement on the left to the type of computer on the right most likely to meet it.

a)	run programs from the 60s, 70s and 80s alongside more modern systems.	i)	PC
b)	run Microsoft Office and Internet Explorer.	ii)	mainframe
c)	provide a lot of processing power cheaply.	iii)	collection of servers

My Mac tells sexist jokes — it's not very PC...

Even consoles like Playstations and Nintendos are microcomputers — but designed specifically for playing games. Dunno why they don't do a GCSE in video games — then you could just spend your practicals grinding on Tony Hawk's, and I could write about that instead...

Networks — LANs and WANs

Q1 Which of the following are advantages of using networks, which are disadvantages, and which are neither?

a) WANs are vulnerable to hackers and viruses.
b) Communication across networks is cheap and fast.
c) She said, "You love to be in love, but you're never really in love."
d) Don't you want me baby? Don't you want me, Oh-woh-oh-oh?
e) Security measures are needed to restrict access to networks.
f) A fault with a server can prevent a whole network from working.
g) It's not what you know, it's who you know that's important.
h) Oooh weeee oooh I look just like Buddy Holly.
i) England is mine, and it owes me a living.
j) Peripherals such as printers can be shared amongst many users.
k) There's a taste in my mouth and it's no taste at all.
l) What will happen in the morning when the world it gets so crowded that you can't look out the window in the morning?
m) Software can be shared amongst different users.
n) High on a hill was a lonely goatherd lay odelay ee odelay ee ho.
o) Cabling can be expensive to install and replace.

"No more," pleaded the cockroach. But the computer only laughed.

Q2 *LANs and WANs are different types of networks.*

a) What does LAN stand for?
b) What does WAN stand for?

Q3 Give one reason why a company might use a WAN.
Give an example of a type of company that would use a WAN.

Q4 What is the dedicated computer called that runs the software needed by a network, and stores the files that users have created?

Q5 Give one advantage and one disadvantage of wireless networks.

Networks — Different Configurations

Q1 What type of network does each of these diagrams represent?

a) 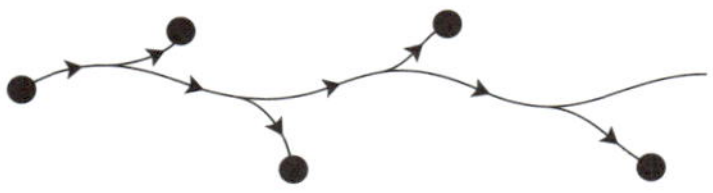

b) 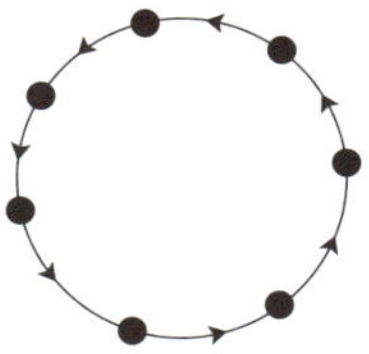

c) 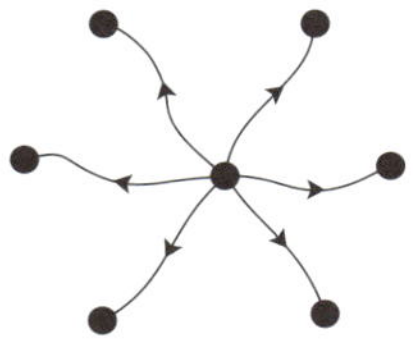

Q2 Give another name for a line network.

Q3 Say whether the following statements about networks are true or false.

a) Line networks are the most expensive.
b) Ring networks are slower than line networks.
c) Star networks give access to a central computer.

Q4 Copy and complete the table below, showing the pros and cons of each type of network.

Network	Pros	Cons
Star	1.	1.
	2.	2.
Line	1.	1.
		2.
Ring	1.	1.
	2.	2.

Q5 Copy and complete these sentences about networks using the words spoken by Georgina.

a) Star networks are used when a ...... number of ...... need to be connected to a central computer. Each workstation is connected ...... to the central computer.

b) In ...... networks ...... is sent to and from the ...... along a line of cable. All terminals are connected to this ....

c) ...... networks are a bit like line networks, except that all the equipment is ...... in a .... Data flows around the network in ...... only.

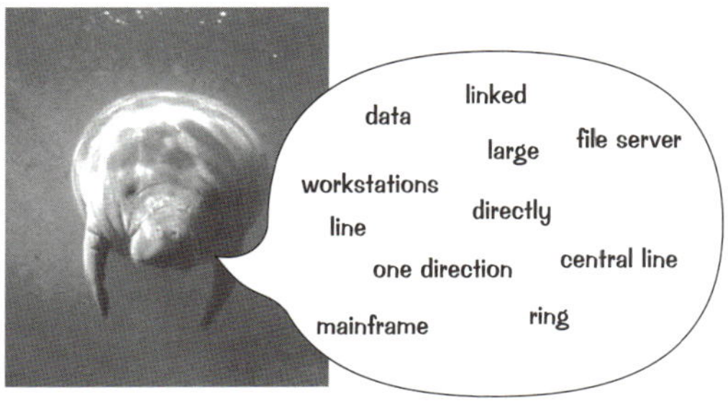

data
linked
large
file server
workstations
directly
line
one direction
central line
mainframe
ring

Note: one word is used twice.

Network Security

Q1 Name the three main types of network security.

Q2 Give six physical security precautions that can be taken to help keep hardware safe.

Q3 Label these diagrams of the ancestral method of file backup:

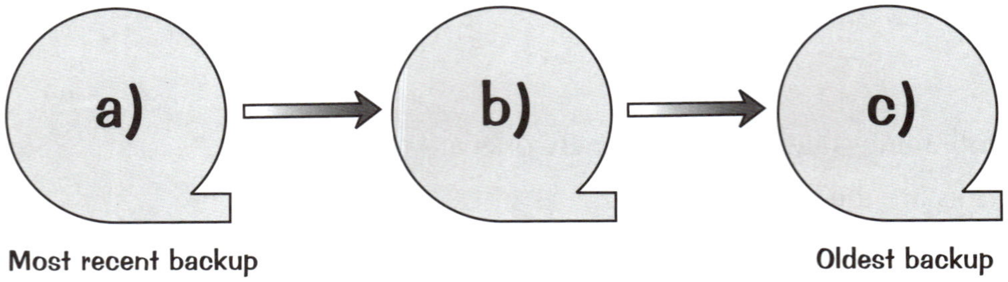

Q4 Fill in the gaps in the paragraph below about the ancestral method of backup. Use the words in the box below the text.

The son is the most ...... backup of the .... When the next ...... is made, this becomes the ....

When the next ...... is made after that, the father ...... the .... The grandfather file is ...... when a new son is ....

So if the ...... file is lost or ...... there are ...... backup files available.

original	becomes	three	recent	backup	created
damaged	backup	file	father	grandfather	deleted

Q5 Write a sentence to define each of these terms:

a) read-only file
b) hidden file
c) archiving

Q6 What are access rights?

Get those grey snails away from me cabbages...

I wonder what David's password for his computer is? And I wonder if Victoria knows it too? Hmmm that is interesting. Almost as interesting as ICT. But not quite. Nothing could be THAT interesting.

Input Devices

Q1 Name the most common input device.

Q2 Copy and complete the following table.

Type of keyboard	Where used	Type of buttons
Qwerty		
Concept		

Q3 *Niall is planning to open a fast food restaurant.*
He needs to install keyboards for staff to use on the checkout.

What type of keyboard would be most appropriate?

Q4 Copy and complete the sentences using words from the box below:

When the .... is over an icon, menu items, or the edge of a picture the mouse buttons can be .... or .... This sends a .... to the computer. The button can also be .... to .... something across the screen. A mouse has an .... that .... how the mouse is moved across a flat surface. From this, the computer can work out the .... and .... the mouse has travelled. This is used to move the .... on the ....

clicked	optical sensor	direction	drag
screen	distance	command	double-clicked
cursor	held down	cursor	detects

Q5 Explain what a touch sensitive pad on a laptop is for and how it works.

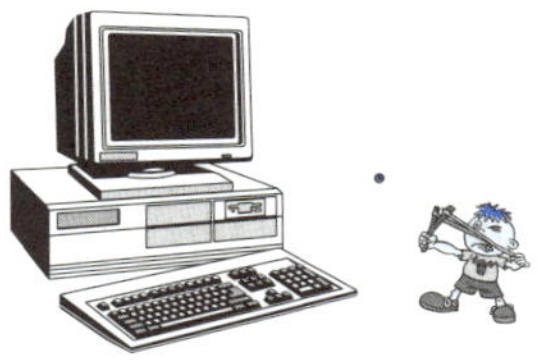

I need input — thank goodness it's lunchtime...

Ah, a beautiful page there about different kinds of keyboards and all sorts of lovely stuff. Not dull at all. And it's already Section Two. I'm so happy. And in denial.

Input Devices

Q1 Copy and complete the following sentences using words from the box below:

A joystick can be used to play computer .... The joystick can be moved a certain .... in any .... The vertical and horizontal changes from its .... position are .... by .... to give a set of ...., which form the .... data.

rest	distance	games
recorded	direction	input
coordinates	sensors	chess

Q2 Say which of the following statements are true and which are false:

a) Scanned images can create very large bitmap files which take up a lot of memory.

b) Scanned images can be easily manipulated with vector graphics software.

c) OCR stands for Optical Character Recognition.

d) Magnetic Ink Character Recognition is used by banks to process the payment of cheques.

e) MICR is very cheap to use although very unreliable.

f) MICR is expensive to use although it is almost 100% accurate.

Q3 Optical Mark Recognition is a useful way of inputting data into a computer. List one advantage and one disadvantage of using this method.

Q4 *A local lottery has decided to invest in computer technology to promote game play. It intends to make use of optical mark recognition (OMR) to enhance its operations.*

What are the advantages to the organisers and players of the game of using OMR, rather than a manual method of reading the numbers? Give one disadvantage.

Input Devices

Q1 Give two different input methods that could be used to do each of the following.

a) record customers' purchases at a supermarket

b) capture video footage and transfer to a computer

c) navigate menus on an MP3 player

Q2 Link the input device to its description, by matching each letter to a number.

a) digital cameras

b) midi instruments

c) sensors

d) touch-sensitive screens

e) video digitisers

f) touch-tone telephones

g) microphones

h) light pens

1) They're a bit like scanners as they save an image as a series of dots called pixels. Most can also record video clips.

2) Used to select from menus or draw directly onto a screen.

3) Used to input data into voice-recognition systems.

4) They're used to record environmental information and convert it into data.

5) They have a different tone for each button on the keypad.

6) They're a bit like concept keyboards but rather than pressing a key you touch the screen.

7) For creating music files where the actual notes, timing and instruments are recorded as digital data.

8) Used to convert analogue video into digital files.

Q3 Which input device does the following statement describe?

The image is saved as a series of dots called pixels and can be uploaded to a computer and edited using photo-editing software.

Forget the light pen — give me a lightsaber...

I've never really understood why they need to give these things fancy names like 'input devices' — just seems to complicate things. Anyway, you need to know all the main ones, along with a bit about how they work. It's all there in the revision guide...

The CPU

Q1 Which of the following does CPU stand for?

a) Common Practice Unit

b) Calculating and Processing Unit

c) Central Processing Unit

d) Control Process Unit

Q2 Choose three statements which describe the main jobs of the CPU.

a) Performs arithmetic.

b) Glows a menacing red colour at night.

c) Ties knots in string.

d) Responds to control signals.

e) Puts funk into a punk.

f) Moves things around in memory.

Q3 Name, and briefly describe two particularly important types of instruction that the CPU deals with.

Q4 Explain, in your own words, what a control signal does.

What does a programmer say when he meets his mates? — "ALU"...

Yup it's tricky, but you've gotta keep going. Imagine you're lost in the desert. It's dry and dusty. A few bones scattered about. There's no water. You're feeling faint. But stop now and you're dead.

Output Devices — Printers

Q1 Copy and complete the table. Write in two advantages, and two disadvantages, for each output device.

Output Device	Advantages	Disadvantages
Dot Matrix Printer		
Laser Printer		

Q2 Write down whether the following statements are true or false.

a) The print head of a laser printer is made up of a matrix of dots.

b) A laser printer uses an ink ribbon while an inkjet printer uses a cartridge.

c) A laser printer etches onto the drum a mirror image of the page to be printed. Ink is attracted onto the negative electrical charge, before the paper is heated and the ink is fused onto it.

d) A dot matrix printer uses different patterns of pins to push the ribbon and its ink onto printer paper.

Q3 Which printers are also referred to as 'impact' printers?

Q4 Choose **a**, **b**, **c** or **d** to complete the following sentence:

Printers are used to...

a) temporarily display data

b) produce permanent hard copies

c) back up data

d) heat paper to a suitable temperature for warming the face

Output Devices — More Printers

Q1 Below are the three main types of printer and some descriptions of when they are used. Link each printer with the description of when it is used, by matching each letter with a number.

a) inkjet printer

b) dot-matrix printer

c) laser printer

1) When you want to print lots of copies of the same text but are not worried about noise, quality and speed.

2) When you want good quality affordable printing but not a lot of it.

3) When you want to print loads of pages of professional quality documents quickly.

Q2 Copy and complete the following sentences using the words in the box below:

Inkjet printers are a good compromise as they cost .... to buy than other printers and produce good quality printouts. The print head of an inkjet device has lots of tiny .... through which small .... of ink are .... onto the paper. In some printers, these are controlled by .... while others .... ink so that it .... and pushes through onto the paper.

less pride expands laser heat
spouts sprayed jets prawns crystals

Q3 Copy and complete the following sentences, using your own words:

a) A printer buffer is...

b) Spooling is...

Q4 *Sarah has decided to buy a new printer. She wants to be able to print both a colour newsletter for a snowboarding club and formal letters to French government officials. She wants to print fifteen copies of each of these, every two months.*

What type of printer would suit Sarah and why?

Dot Matrix — she plays Keanu Reeves' mother...

Did you know that an old meaning of the word "matrix" comes from 16th century Italian and means "the womb"? If you care about this kind of thing, make sure you do English at A-level. I'd hazard a guess a career as a systems analyst isn't for you.

Other Kinds of Output Device

Q1 **Explain the role of a Visual Display Unit.**

Q2 **Explain the relative advantages of CRT and LCD monitors.**

Q3 **Copy and complete the following sentences using the words in the box:**

Graph Plotters are specialised .... and are .... and .... for drawing architect plans. A .... plotter holds paper on a flat surface and a plotter .... moves over it from left to right. On the plotter arm is a ...., which moves up and down the piece of paper.

accurate arm flat-bed VDU
printers holder pen precise prime

Q4 *Jason is the manager of an architectural business and employs a team of four staff who help complete scale drawings for building plans. Jason's business doesn't have any type of output device to print these plans, so he wants to invest in a suitable printer.*

Suggest the type of printer that would best suit his needs and explain why.

Q5 **Computers can use speech synthesis to produce artificial human-sounding voices. Explain two possible uses of this.**

Other Kinds of Output Device

Q1 a) Microfilm is a type of output device. Describe how it stores information.

b) Name the hardware device you would use to view Microfilm.

Q2 a) Write down two advantages for using Microfilm instead of paper.

b) Write down two disadvantages of using Microfilm rather than paper.

Q3 Name two output devices that could be used on a burglar alarm system.

Q4 Copy and complete the following sentence by selecting a, b or c from the list below:

Actuators are...

a) output devices that are able to move and perform simple mechanical tasks.
b) storage devices that send signals to the CPU.
c) output devices which send instructions to the control interface.

Q5 Describe the difference between a stepper-motor and a servo-motor.

Q6 Copy and complete the following sentences using the words in the box below:

Hydraulic actuators are powered by .... pressure controlled by the computer.
They are .... but powerful.

Pneumatic actuators are like hydraulic ones but are powered by .... pressure instead.
They are less powerful but more ....

plant responsive fluid
aqueous air fire wind
slow fast nippy

Q7 Provide an example of an operation or process which uses a pneumatic actuator.

Output devices — worth a hill of beans in a crazy world...

"Pneumatic actuator"? Did I really ask a question about a pneumatic actuator? Sorry.
Ah well, I suppose you do need to know all this stuff — I'm doing you a favour really.

Data Storage — ROM and RAM

Q1 What does RAM stand for?

Q2 What does ROM stand for?

Q3 Say which of the following statements are true and which are false.

A All data that is stored in volatile RAM is lost if the electrical power is switched off.

B The user can write new data or programs to ROM.

C ROM stores data and programs essential for the computer to start.

D Non-volatile RAM is slower than volatile RAM.

E ROM and RAM are backing storage on the hard drive.

F Flash memory is an example of volatile memory.

Q4 Copy and complete the sentences using the words in the box below:

Volatile RAM stores data as .... electrical signals and users should learn to .... their work regularly as data stored in the RAM will be lost if the electrical power is switched off. ROM is .... memory, so it's a type of .... memory.

temporary save salsa computerised
non-volatile volatile resistance save permanent

The ram looked cute, but really he was volatile.

RAM, a RAM, A Ram — a-Ram a-Lam a-Ding Dong...

I know this RAM and ROM stuff seems pretty basic, but you've really got to have all the meanings and stuff sorted if you want to move onto the trickier stuff. Go on. You know it makes sense.

Data Storage — Backing Storage

Q1 Copy and complete the following table:

Storage device	Advantage	Disadvantage
Hard disk		
Optical disk		

Q2 Complete the following sentences using words from the box below:

.... disks are usually found inside computers and are .... circular plates that have been .... hard drives can also be connected if additional storage is needed. An .... disk stores digital data as small .... on a reflective surface. A .... moves across the surface of the disk to read the data.

optical	hard	indentations	digit	
backup	envelope	magnetised	inhibited	
rigid	tab	external	internal	laser-beam

Q3 Give an advantage of using optical disks over magnetic tapes.

Q4 Compare the storage capacity of CDs, DVDs and 3.5 inch floppy disks.

Q5 How many times can you write data onto a CD-R?

I was rude to my hard disk — I really got his backup...

OK this is a bit technical, but data storage is pretty fundamental to anyone using a computer. If you can't store what you've done, you may as well have used a typewriter. My point being... what was my point... ah, yes... because it's so important, you're bound to get a question on it.

Data Storage — Backing Storage

Q1 Match each the following types of disk to the correct statement on the right:

a) CD-ROM

b) CD-R

c) CD-RW

i) Once data has been written onto them, they become read-only discs.

ii) Once data has been written onto them, it can subsequently be deleted and replaced with different data.

iii) It can only be used to read, not record, data.

Q2 a) What do the initials DVD stand for?

b) What is the name of a DVD you can write data to?

Q3 Give two examples of storage media that use flash memory.

Q4 Give some advantages and disadvantages of using flash memory cards and sticks.

Q5 Describe how magnetic tape is used.

How can we be lost? I thought you had the directions on a stick?

Operating Systems — Main Tasks

Q1 Explain what is meant by the term **operating system**.

Q2 Say whether the following statements about the tasks of operating systems are true or false.

a) Operating systems enable applications software to communicate with the system's hardware

b) They prevent applications from operating.

c) They enable applications to operate.

d) They manage system resources.

e) They operate utilities such as print managers and virus scanning software.

f) They notify the users of ways in which they could work more efficiently.

Q3 Explain some features of the following OS types in your own words.

a) Single Program

b) Multi-tasking

c) Multi-user

Q4 Copy and complete the following sentences using the words below.

Operating systems also maintain system .... are prevented from accessing each other's .... Users can only access resources (such as individual files) if they have .... Extra users can be added to the system and their permissions restricted by the system ....

programs	**administrator**	**security**	**written consent**
resources	**temperature**	**disk drives**	**permission**

Operating Systems — User Interfaces

Q1 What is meant by the term **user interface**?

Q2 Name three types of user interfaces.

Q3 Copy and complete the sentences, using the words in the box below:

A .... presents the user with a blank screen while a .... system displays a list of options organised under various .... or .... The most popular type of system used today is a .... interface, which combines a menu-driven interface with .... to represent the main commands.

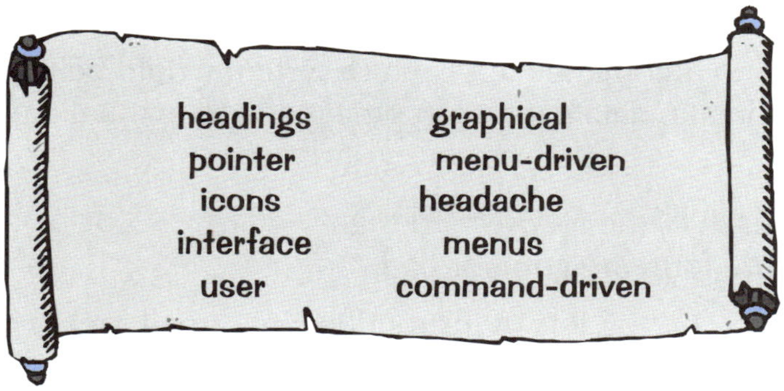

Q4 What does the term **WIMPs** stand for when talking about a graphical user interface?

Q5 Which of the following features are important to think about when designing a GUI?

a) Modelling your new interface on existing styles so the user can quickly learn how it use it.

b) Using colour and sound to help the user navigate through the system.

c) How the GUI will be output, once the developing stage is completed.

d) Using on-line help to enable the user to find out how to perform various tasks.

e) Any of the following: food, shopping, sport, TV, home time.

Those were the days, my friend — I thought the section would never end...

Data Capture

Q1 In which part of the "input → process → output" cycle does data capture occur?

a) Input b) Process c) Output

Q2 Data capture forms can be filled in by placing a tick in the right box (like on a school register). The forms can then be read by an OMR reader. What do the initials OMR stand for?

Q3 For the four methods of data capture below, say whether the method of data capture is manual, automatic, or semi-automatic.

i) Questionnaire
ii) Sensor
iii) Bar code reader
iv) Computer-generated form

Q4 List two advantages of using each of the following:

a) Automatic data capture systems
b) Manual data capture systems

Q5 Choose one area where an automatic data capture system would be used and describe why you would use automatic data capture in preference to manual data capture.

Q6 Say whether you think each of the following design features for a data capture form are **good** or **bad**.

a) cluttered
b) uncluttered
c) complex
d) simple
e) lots of instructions in a small font
f) simple instructions in a large font
g) plenty of space for answers
h) pictures of frogs and toads

Q7 Name two things you should do with a completed form design before using it to collect data.

Q8 The form shown below has been designed to collect information for a games console club. The club needs to collect the following information:

name, address, post code, telephone number, type of games console used, date of birth, signature, and guardian's signature if the member is under 16

a) List five things that are wrong with the design of this form.

b) Design your own form for the club and correct the bad design features you listed in a) above.

ACME GAMES CONSOLE CLUB

What is your name? ____________________

Address:..
....
....
....

When were you born? ____________________

What games console do you own? ____________

Signature:
Guardian's signature:

Data Validation and Verification

Q1 Complete the following sentence by selecting **a**, **b**, **c** or **d** from the list below:

Data validation checks make sure that:

a) the data is entered in the correct place.
b) the data is the same as the original data.
c) the data is the correct type and format.
d) the data is saved.

Q2 Write down the names of three types of data validation check.

Q3 Copy and complete the following sentence by selecting **a**, **b**, **c** or **d** from the list below:

Data verification ensures that the data entered into the computer is:

a) the correct length.
b) the correct type.
c) secure.
d) the same as the original data.

Q4 The data verification process of entering data twice is called:

a) Presence check
b) Proof-reading
c) Double-entry
d) Data validation

Q5 a) Write down 1 advantage of data validation checks.

b) Write down 2 disadvantages of data validation checks.

c) Write down 2 disadvantages of data verification checks.

Q6 Use a full A4 page to draw a table with the following headings:

Name of check	Description	Validation	Verification

In the "name of check" column put the following:

Data type check
Proof-reading
Range check
Length check
Check digit
Double-entry
Presence check

Leave plenty of space between the name of each check.

Enter a description of how each check works in the "Description" column. Finally, place a tick in the appropriate column to show whether it's a validation or verification check.

Data Storage

Q1 Blocks of data organised and stored under one name by computer systems are called:

a) directories
b) fields
c) files
d) records

Q2 Say which of the following is another name for a directory:

a) database
b) folder
c) file
d) hard disk

Q3 Say which of the statements below are true and which are false.

A A field is a type of file.
B A file can have several names.
C A file extension can be used to tell the operating system which program to use to open the file.
D File extensions are extra information placed before the file name.
E Files can be stored on the computer's hard drive.

Q4 *The hierarchy diagram shows how a database file is made up from records and fields.*

a) Draw the diagram below on a piece of paper and fill in the empty boxes to show where the records and fields appear in the diagram:

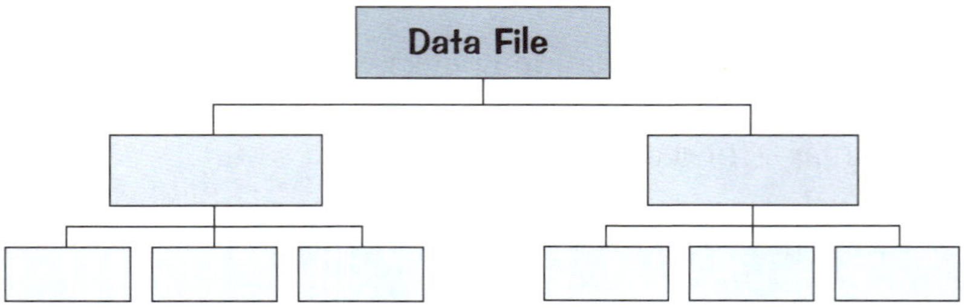

b) Add an extra box to your diagram to show where directories belong in the hierarchy and label the box "Directory".

Q5 Use your own words to describe each of the following data storage concepts:

a) a directory
b) fixed-length records
c) variable-length records

We want to see the wizard — sorry, this is ICT, not OZ...

Here's a gag for all you binary freaks: 0101010101010000100101101001001010010100001110110110110 11 01011101010. Then the vicar says "0011!#*!10010". 1001001010 (this last bit is hysterical binary laughter).

Data Processing

Q1 Match the name of the data processing type to the descriptions given below:

1) Processing carried out as a single action that will either succeed or fail completely.

2) Responds seemingly instantly to changes in input data.

3) Lots of different updates (jobs) are stored up and all processed together.

4) The computer responds to user requests made through a suitable interface, e.g. a GUI or series of prompts.

A) Interactive processing

B) Transaction processing

C) Batch processing

D) Real-time processing

Q2 For each of the following sentences, say whether they are describing an advantage or a disadvantage.

a) Real-time processing can be expensive.
b) Interactive processing allows operators to interrogate the computer system to find things like free seats in a cinema on a given date and time.
c) There is a time delay in batch processing, as information is stored up and files are updated at night or at weekends.
d) Information is updated immediately in a real-time data processing system.
e) Large volumes of data are processed efficiently by batch processing systems.
f) Interactive systems give the user control of what the computer does.

Q3 Copy out the table below and fill in the "type of processing" column with the appropriate name — real-time, batch, transaction or interactive.

Task	Type of Processing
Aircraft cockpit display	
Booking seats in a theatre	
Cancelling a magazine subscription	
Calculating the wages for a large company	
Looking at the availability of goods in a shop	
Controlling traffic lights in a city	
Producing 1000s of end of month customer bills	
Subscribing to a monthly video and CD club	

Q4 In your own words, describe what is meant by the following terms:

a) Interactive processing
b) Transaction processing
c) Batch processing
d) Real-time processing

Accessing and Updating Data

Q1 Serial data access is different from sequential data access because:

a) the computer can go directly to sequential records.
b) in sequential data access records are sorted into order.
c) in serial data access records are sorted into order.
d) the computer can go directly to serial records.

Q2 Complete the diagram below by drawing lines between each data access type, and the storage medium/media it can be used with. Use these two facts to help you:

1) Files on magnetic tape can only be read by being played from start to finish.
2) Direct data access can only be done if the file is stored on a direct storage medium.

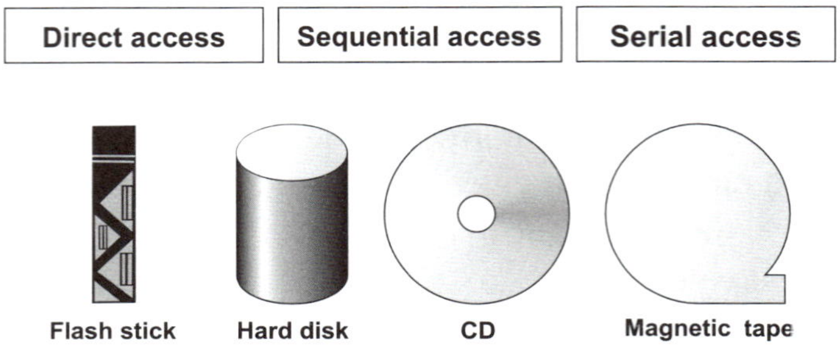

Q3 Below are two "disadvantages". For each disadvantage, write down the method of data access that it applies to — serial, sequential or direct.

a) High-capacity disk storage media are usually more expensive than the same capacity magnetic tape.
b) As every record has to be read in order to find the one to be updated, seeking a random record can be slow.

Q4 The sentences below describe the process of updating a sequential file, but are in the wrong order. Put the sentences into the correct order.

a) The master file and transaction file are combined.
b) The records that have changed are sorted into order.
c) The records that have changed are written to a transaction file.

Q5 How does the process of updating a direct access file differ from the process of updating a sequential file?

Data Presentation

Q1 What type of device is used to present data to the users of computer systems?

a) storage device
b) input device
c) output device

Q2 Which item from the list below would be needed to include sound in a multimedia presentation?

a) monitor
b) keyboard
c) mouse
d) speaker
e) scanner
f) printer
g) graphics card
h) plotter

In the year 2086 elite gangs of computer-busters roam the city streets.

Q3 List four different ways that information can be presented to users of a computer system.

Q4 Explain what is meant by the term "hard copy".

Q5 Copy and complete the table below by adding two advantages and two disadvantages of using screen displays and hard copies to present information to the users of a computer system.

Output Device	Advantages	Disadvantages
Screen Displays		
Hard Copy		

Q6 Explain what is meant by the term "WYSIWYG".

Data tattoos and piercings are frowned upon...

This stuff might seem basic, but then again, 'not wearing shell-suits' seems pretty basic as well and people still tragically muck that up. So get this right or it'll lead to shell-suits. You've been warned.

Step One — Identify the Problem

Q1 Write a sentence explaining what the term **systems analysis** means.

Q2 The diagram below shows the System Life Cycle.
Copy and complete the diagram by filling in the gaps.

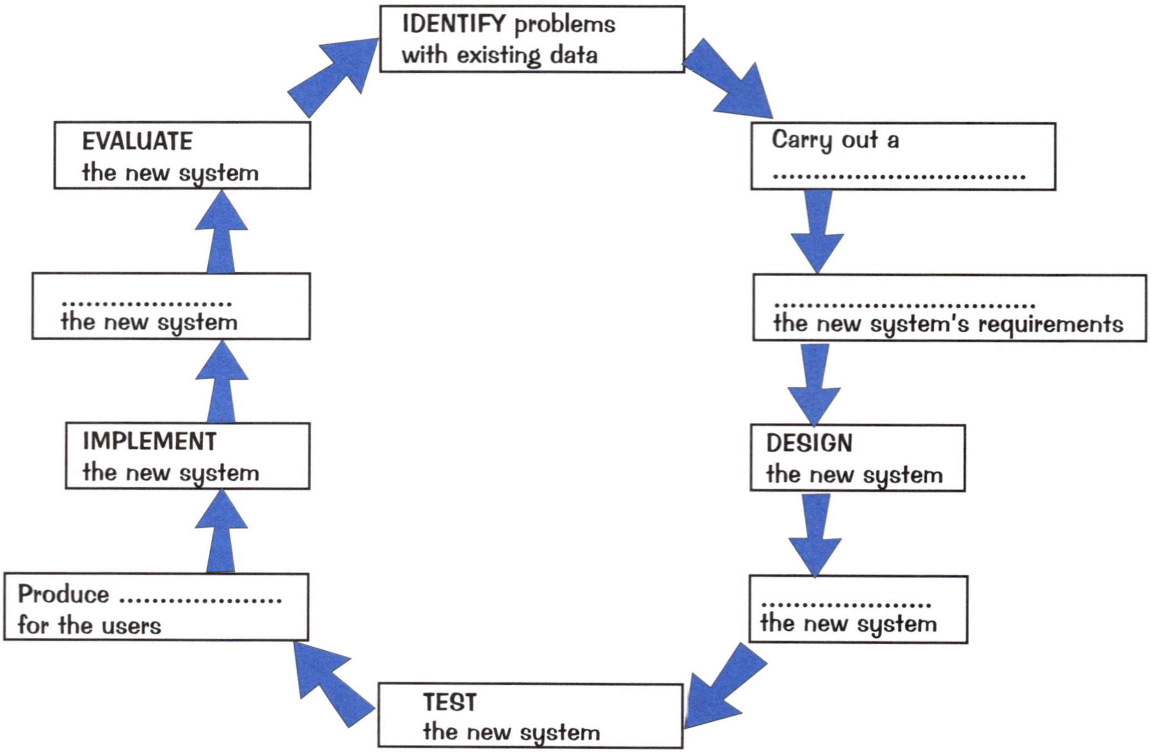

Q3 What are the two main problems usually found with existing systems?

Q4 What four things does a systems analyst do to identify the problems with a system?

Q5 In your experience, are systems analysts normally:

a) happy, well-rounded individuals?

b) the person who comes round to fix the computer system?

c) crazy as a woodlouse high on ant powder?

Step Two — greet the problem and make small talk...

If the problem is too much cheesecake, don't panic, just eat it and move on. If the problem's system-based, things are a bit trickier and eating is unlikely to bring about a satisfactory resolution.

Analysis — The Feasibility Study

Q1 What is the purpose of a feasibility study?

Q2 Name the four stages of a feasibility study.

Q3 Read the following statements about the objectives of a feasibility study, and write down whether each one is true or false.

a) Objectives are standardised outcomes for new systems, that are used to test whether a new system functions properly.

b) Objectives are specific outcomes for new systems, that are used to test whether a new system does what it was originally intended to do.

c) An alternative name for objectives is data spell criteria.

d) Objectives are also called evaluation criteria.

e) New systems should never have more than one objective.

Q4 Copy and complete the following sentences using words from the box below.

As part of the .... study the systems analyst needs to make .... about the types of .... and software that will be used in the new system. These choices might be .... later on, when he moves onto the .... stage of the system life cycle.

feasibility hardware evaluation computerised
ingenuity design changed reversed
construction pulverised decisions

Q5 What is the purpose of doing a cost-benefit study?

Q6 Who does the systems analyst usually present his findings and recommendations to?

Design — Input, Process, Output

Q1 Write down whether the following parts of the design process relate to the input, process or output.

a) Decide how to present the information.

b) Decide how the data needs to be structured.

c) Decide how the data will be validated.

d) Write the commands that enable the tasks to be done.

e) Design the data capture forms.

f) Produce a plan to test if the processing works.

Q2 Write down whether the following statements are true or false.

a) The use of codes in input data increases file size but enables computerised processing of the information.

b) N-processed data should be sketched to show what the user will see when they input the data into the system.

c) The tasks that the system needs to perform should be based on the original problem and objectives.

Q3 Copy and complete the following sentences using words from the box below:

It is important for the output of a system to be ....
Users should only be shown the .... that they need.
It should be laid out in a format that they can ....
The layout of .... and printouts should first be .... in rough.
The rough sketches should then be shown to the .... to check they are alright.

understand in code user
modelled numbered user-friendly
output screens processing screens
commands sketched information

Design — Top-Down and Data-Flow

Q1 *Look at the diagram and answer the questions below.*

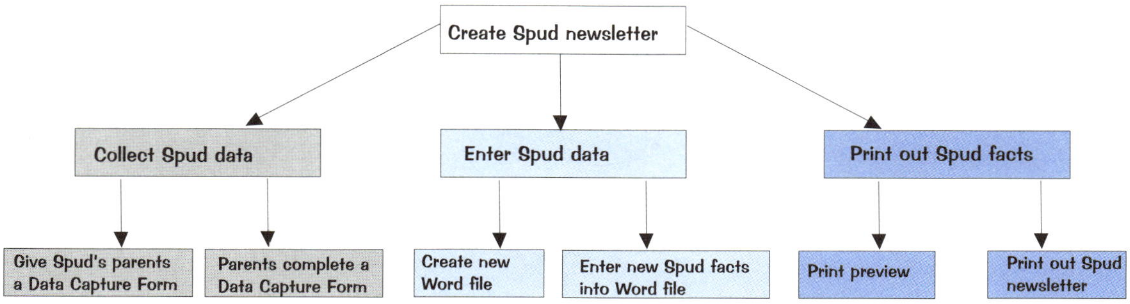

a) What is this type of diagram called?

b) How can you tell what order the tasks should be done in?

c) Does the diagram break smaller tasks down into bigger tasks?

Q2 What information about a system is shown in a data-flow diagram?

Q3 Here are three symbols used in data-flow diagrams. Explain what each one means.

a) 

b) 

c) 

Q4 Do data-flow diagrams show the hardware and software used in a system?

Top down — for windy convertibles and rude women...

Take a deep cleansing breath, then go read the newspaper, do the crossword and have a bath. My Yoga teacher would suggest imagining a petal and every detail of the petal. Don't do that.

Design — System Flowcharts

Q1 What information about a system is shown in a system flowchart?

Q2 Look at the diagram and answer the questions below:

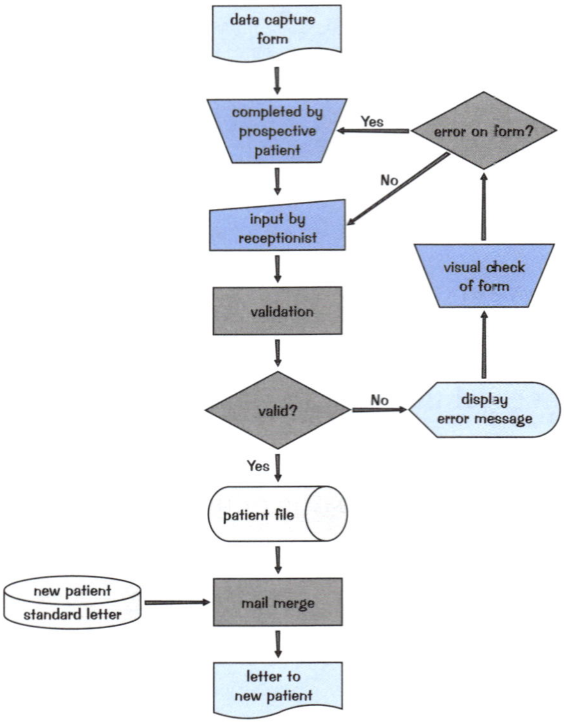

a) What type of disk is the new patient standard letter on?

b) Is 'error on form' a process, a decision or a visual display?

c) Describe what happens to the data if it is found to be invalid.

Q3 Copy out the symbols below, and label what each one means.

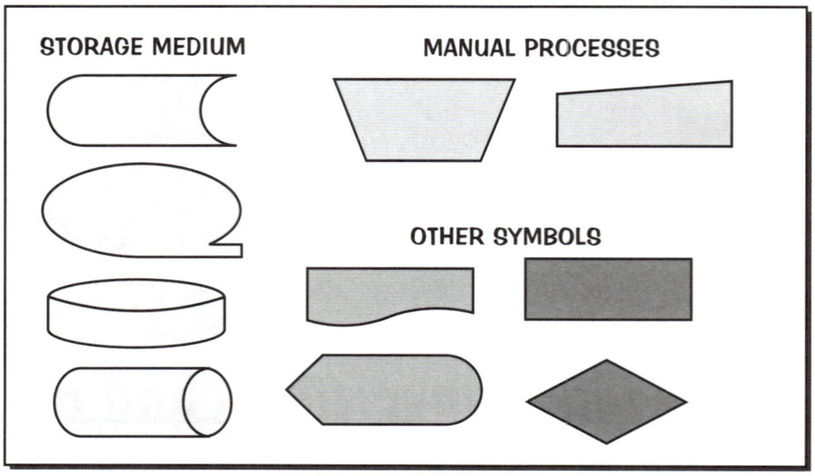

Testing and User Documentation

Q1 What is the purpose of system testing?

Q2 Explain the three types of test data used in system testing.

Q3 What is acceptance testing?

Jack had failed the
acceptance testing
again...

Q4 Copy and complete the table, by filling in the second column.

Type of user documentation	Description
Installation guides	
User guides	
Tutorials	

Q5 Why do technical documents contain more complex language and diagrams than user documents?

Q6 Describe two instances when technical documentation would be useful.

Everybody's free to feel good...

Ok, so you've read the paper, had a bath and done the crossword. Now it's full on ICT time — keep your eyelids pinned back and your brain revving until you know these pages inside out. Ok... OK?

Implementation and Evaluation

Q1 What is implementation?

Q2 Name the three types of implementation.

Q3 Copy the table and complete it by filling in the blank spaces.

Type of implementation	Advantage	Disadvantage
	Time for the new system to be fully tested.	
Direct implementation		
		All the tasks need to be done twice.

Q4 Copy and complete the sentences using words from the box below.

Once a new system is installed it will be .... to see whether it's working properly. How well it's working will be regularly .... to check that the system still meets its .... Evaluation involves .... and .... users and studying printouts. The system might run into problems if the .... increases. If the system can no longer cope the .... begins again.

monitored	objectives	workload
evaluated	engaging	interviewing
dampened	observing	system life cycle

I would like to apologise...

OK, so ICT is not so bad and my blood pressure is returning to normal now. And — pom pom pom de-dah — you've finished another section.

page 28 page 30 page 32

Word Processing Basics

Q1 Copy and complete the following sentence by selecting **a** or **b** from the list below:

Modern word processors are more powerful...

a) ...because they can combine graphics, text and numerical information.

b) ...than you can ever imagine.

Q2 Copy and complete the following sentences by choosing the correct words from the box:

editing	formatting	processed

Text entered into word processors can be .... easily.
You can change the appearance — called text ...., and change the content — called text ....

Q3 Explain briefly what word processing templates are used for.

Q4 List five different types of document that you'd expect a word processor to have a template for.

Q5 *Look at the block of text below and answer the questions which follow it:*

> *Apparently if you were to let an infinite number of monkeys type for an infinite number of hours they would eventually produce three Shakespeare plays, one CGP revision guide and the script for a complete new series of Buffy. Unfortunately no one has yet been able to find an infinite number of monkeys willing to take part in an experiment to test this theory as they are all already tied up working for CGP.*

Explain the problem with the text with reference to each of these features:

a) colour

b) underlining

c) font

Q6 What is the golden rule when using a word processor to avoid the problems described in Q5?

Hint — the answer's simple

Monkey see — monkey do...

It's true — word processors make writing stuff so easy that even a chimp could do it. But of course there's no way a chimp could write a workbook. That's just ridiculous. Now pass me a banana.

Text Formatting and Editing

Q1 Copy and complete the following sentence by selecting **a** or **b** from the list below:

Serifs are:

a) the little twiddly bits at the tops and bottoms of characters.

b) American officers of the law with lisps.

Q2 Draw two columns and label them 'serif' and 'sans serif'.
Write the letter of each example in the correct column.

(A) Is it serif or isn't it — place bets now.

(B) What about this — quick, is it serif?

(C) Well, come on, place bets.

(D) Is it serif or isn't it — betting ends.

Q3 Briefly explain how you would copy a piece of text so it appeared more than once on a page.

Q4 Briefly explain what page margins are.

Q5 Copy and complete the following sentences, choosing the correct words from the box:

indenting	line spacing	margins	TAB

.... is when you start a paragraph away from the side of the page.
This can be done using the .... key.

.... fix how far from the side of the page the text starts and finishes.

.... adjusts how far apart the lines of text are.

Q6 Match each type of alignment (a to c) its example on the right.

a) Left-aligned

b) Right-aligned

c) Centre-aligned

Sentence 1: It's me, is it not obvious.

Sentence 2: Don't talk rubbish, it's me.

Sentence 3: Come on Nigel, pick me.

Improving Presentation

Q1 Copy and complete the following sentences, choosing the correct words from the box.

break up	tables	columns	automatically

.... are a good way to present lists of numerical or textual information. Putting borders around tables can .... the information. You can use .... which flow down the page and .... jump to the next page.

Q2 a) What paper size are the pages in this book?

b) Are they landscape or portrait?

Q3 a) Copy the sketch below of a double page, and label the widow and the orphan.

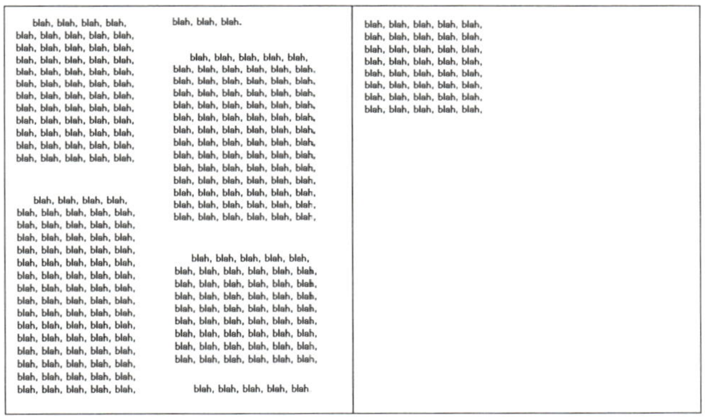

b) Suggest two ways in which you could get rid of the widow and orphan.

Q4 a) What does WYSIWYG stand for?

b) Explain what WYSIWYG means.

c) Give a reason why some views in a WYSIWYG program may be non-WYSIWYG.

Keep your hair on — it's only a whizzi-wig...

Now you've got the hang of text formatting, tables, borders, page set-ups and widows and orphans you could lay this page out yourself. Pop in any time you fancy...

Word Processing — Advanced Features

Q1 a) Briefly explain why headers and footers are useful.

b) Copy out the footer on this page.

Q2 Explain the difference between 'search' and 'replace'.

Q3 a) Write TRUE or FALSE for each of these statements:

i) If the spell-checker queries an actual word, you can add it to the dictionary.

ii) Because of spell-checkers you no longer need to know how to spell yourself.

iii) Spell-checkers will only recognise misspelt words — not their context.

iv) A bird in the hand is worth two in the bush.

v) Spell-checkers only come in one language.

vi) A spell-checker will always know which witch is which.

vii) American English and British English are exactly the same.

b) Briefly explain the problems with relying on a grammar-checker.

Q4 Copy and complete the following sentences, choosing the correct words from the box:

score	words	grammar checks	sentences	lengths	readability

As well as checking spelling and grammar, word processors can assess the .... of documents.
The computer counts things like .... of .... and ...., and uses them to calculate an overall ....

Meryl the pig has a readability score of 209

Choose ICT...

Choose headers and footers, choose search and replace, choose spell checking, grammar checking, readability scores — I chose not to choose ICT, I chose life.

Word Processing — Advanced Features

Q1 What are the two items combined by a mail merge?

Q2 Below is an example of a standard letter for a mail merge.
Copy and complete the labels to explain how the mail merge will work.

inserting	database	standard letter	field	merges

Dear <complainer name>

I read with interest your recent letter enquiring about a possible mistake in our Encyclopedia of People with Stereotypical Names. However, I can assure you that you are very much mistaken. It is company policy to always be right. We have checked the error and decided that as we are always right the only explanation is that in this situation we are also right.

Therefore we can only say ya boo sucks to you and suggest that you keep your complaints to yourself in future.

Yours sincerely
Mr I. M. Wright,
Customer Services

'complainer name' is a .... in a .... containing the names of all the complainers.

This .... is linked to the database, and software .... the data by .... each name in the database into the letter.

Q3 Write TRUE or FALSE for each of these statements:

a) A macro is a time-saving device.
b) Macro cheese is a tasty pasta snack.
c) A macro is a sequence of commands stored by the computer.
d) Macros always have long file names.
e) You can run a macro by typing a code.

Q4 a) Explain what is meant by importing.

b) What must you make sure of for imported data to work?

c) What is the difference between embedding and linking?

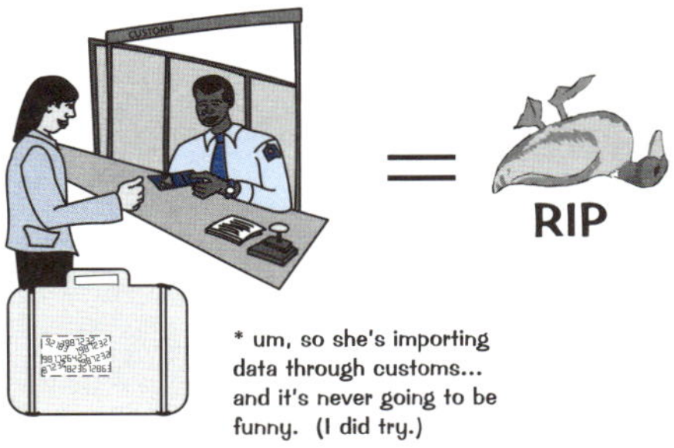

* um, so she's importing data through customs... and it's never going to be funny. (I did try.)

Graphics — Creating Images

Q1 Draw a table with two columns. Label one 'painting software' and the other 'drawing software'. Write each of the following facts in the correct column.

also known as pixel-based software

to edit the image you basically alter each dot individually

graphic saved as a series of coloured dots in a file called a bitmap

also called object based or vector-based software

image saved as coordinates and equations

image edited by manipulating objects

Q2 a) Briefly describe what clipart is.

b) Explain one problem with using the Internet as a source of free images.

Q3 Copy and complete the following sentences, choosing the correct word(s) from each pair:

A JPEG is a [compressed / expanded] bitmap. The disadvantage of making a JPEG is that you lose some of the [picture quality / sound effects]. However, the loss in quality is usually [not / very] noticeable to the human eye. Compressing the image in this way can massively [increase / decrease] the [file's eyes / file size].

Q4 a) What does resolution mean?

b) Explain what effects resolution has on picture quality and file size.

Q5 *There are two main ways to capture images digitally.*
For each way below explain briefly how it works.
Include what sort of images they are used for and how the images are stored.

a) Scanners

b) Digital cameras

Graphics — Manipulating Vector Images

Q1 a) How do you normally resize an image?

b) Write down the letter of the image below that has been resized without keeping the same proportions.

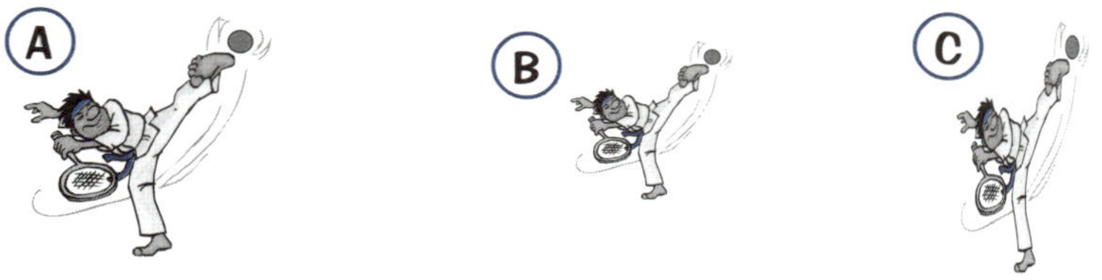

Q2 What could you do if you wanted an image of a snake biting a judge but only had an image of a snake biting a stick of celery?

Q3 For each image below, write down the correct manipulation from the box.

a)

b)

c)

d)

rotating	resizing
recolouring	flipping

Imagine there's no heaven — there's only Grimsby...

You can see how useful graphics and image manipulation are just by looking at this page. We've certainly used all the tricks of the trade for this one — rotating, resizing, recolouring... there's even a man playing the double bass on the back of an elephant — now you're having fun.

Graphics — Manipulating Bitmap Images

Q1 Which of the following statements about pixels are true?

a) A pixel is a coloured dot.
b) A pixel is an angry spot.
c) Thousands of pixels make up any one bitmap image.
d) Each pixel is saved individually.
e) Pixels is what pixies call other pixies who are a lot smaller than they are.
f) To edit an image you need software with tools for changing the pixels.

Q2 For each of the following histograms, say whether it represents an image that is mostly light, mostly dark, or neither.

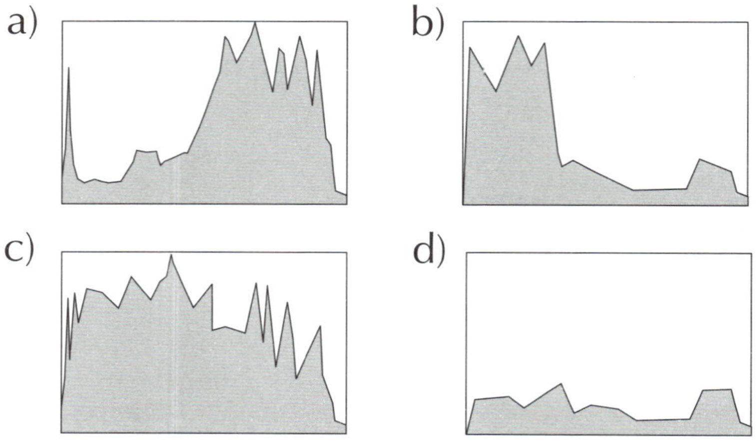

Q3 Describe how bitmap software can manipulate an image that is:

a) Out of focus
b) Too light or too dark

Q4 What does it mean to make an image "grayscale"?

Carole couldn't believe she'd thought "Byte Watchers" was a good idea.

Graphics — Manipulating Bitmap Images

Q1 Match the selection tools to their descriptions:

a) Marquee Select

b) Lasso Select

c) Edge Detection

i) The user draws a shape with the cursor, and all the pixels inside are selected.

ii) The user clicks inside a shape, and the computer tries to find its edges automatically.

iii) The user drags out a rectangle, and the area inside the rectangle is then selected.

Q2 Give a disadvantage for each selection method from Q1.

Steven hadn't meant to marquee select his whole family.

Q3 How can you add objects into a photograph?

Q4 Define the clone tool in your own words.

Q5 Copy and complete the following paragraph using the correct words from the box.

When you're cloning to remove objects, you place a .... brush on what you want to copy, then .... somewhere else. The source brush will move in the same way as the mouse cursor. Anything under the source brush will be copied to the location of the cursor. The tool can be used to copy simple .... such as .... or the .... This is particularly useful when replacing an object with a single colour would look wrong. The clone tool can also .... small areas of the image, such as facial .... or bits of landscape left behind when an object is .... By cloning lots of small pieces, you can even construct ....

paint	patterns	grass	removed
pixies	pieces	repair	new shapes
source	sky	copied	blemishes

Conquer bitmaps — and never be lost again...

With graphics, that is. Bitmaps are no use to you if you get lost in the middle of, say...Pond..thwaite. In the dark. Especially as I made it up — you'd have to be pretty unlucky to actually get stuck there. But seriously — don't want to get lost in the exam? Learn how software can manipulate bitmaps.

Graphics — Computer-Aided Design

Q1 What does CAD stand for?

Q2 Copy and complete these paragraphs explaining the four main uses of CAD:

materials	processed	cost	calculations	designed	components	simulate

Objects can be .... in two dimensions and then .... into a three-dimensional design.

.... can be performed — e.g. calculating the turning circle of a car or the .... of producing it based on standard costs of parts.

Some CAD software can suggest suitable .... and .... for a particular job.

Some CAD software can .... how the object will perform under certain conditions.

Q3 Write TRUE or FALSE for each of these statements:

a) CAD lets you create designs very quickly.

b) It's slow to change designs.

c) CAD software is very cheap.

d) CAD is very simple so users need very little training.

e) Good systems can produce high-resolution images.

f) Simulations help you design better products first time round.

g) CAD software runs well on all computers and doesn't require powerful hardware.

Q4 Copy and complete the table below using the statements in Q3, rewriting the FALSE statements where necessary.

Advantages of CAD	Disadvantages of CAD

Desktop Publishing — Basics

Q1 Copy and complete the following sentences, choosing the correct words from each pair:

> Desktop publishing software is used to build [professional / unprofessional] looking pages. Pages are built up with [frames / drawings] which can contain [text / programs] or [macros / graphics]. You can create text and graphics using the DTP software, but it is often [better / worse] to create the source material in other [larger / specialised] packages.

Q2 a) Information is put on the page in blocks. What are these blocks called?

b) Briefly explain the advantage of using these blocks.

Q3 Copy and complete the labels on these diagrams, using the words from the box.

frame	delete	drag	position	frame-based	move up

With DTP each block of text or picture forms its own .... that you can .... around separately.

Most word processors are not .... so the .... of one thing depends on the position of everything else.

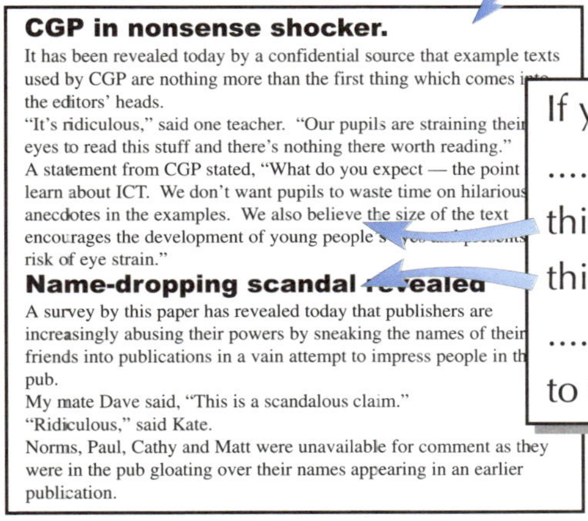

CGP in nonsense shocker.
It has been revealed today by a confidential source that example texts used by CGP are nothing more than the first thing which comes into the editors' heads.
"It's ridiculous," said one teacher. "Our pupils are straining their eyes to read this stuff and there's nothing there worth reading."
A statement from CGP stated, "What do you expect — the point learn about ICT. We don't want pupils to waste time on hilarious anecdotes in the examples. We also believe the size of the text encourages the development of young people's risk of eye strain."
Name-dropping scandal revealed
A survey by this paper has revealed today that publishers are increasingly abusing their powers by sneaking the names of their friends into publications in a vain attempt to impress people in th pub.
My mate Dave said, "This is a scandalous claim."
"Ridiculous," said Kate.
Norms, Paul, Cathy and Matt were unavailable for comment as they were in the pub gloating over their names appearing in an earlier publication.

If you .... this, this will .... to take it's place.

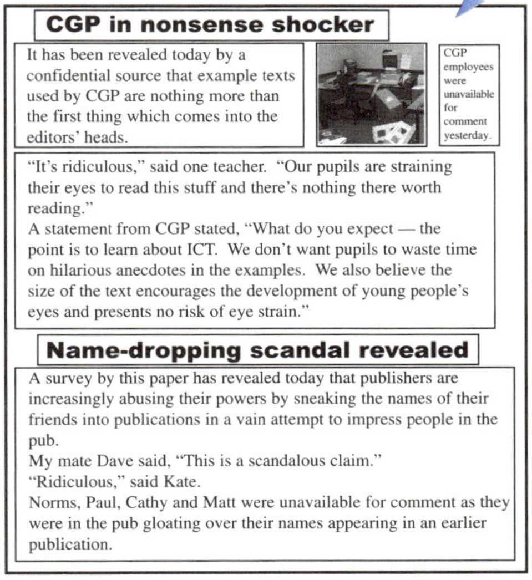

CGP in nonsense shocker
It has been revealed today by a confidential source that example texts used by CGP are nothing more than the first thing which comes into the editors' heads.
CGP employees were unavailable for comment yesterday.
"It's ridiculous," said one teacher. "Our pupils are straining their eyes to read this stuff and there's nothing there worth reading."
A statement from CGP stated, "What do you expect — the point is to learn about ICT. We don't want pupils to waste time on hilarious anecdotes in the examples. We also believe the size of the text encourages the development of young people's eyes and presents no risk of eye strain."
Name-dropping scandal revealed
A survey by this paper has revealed today that publishers are increasingly abusing their powers by sneaking the names of their friends into publications in a vain attempt to impress people in the pub.
My mate Dave said, "This is a scandalous claim."
"Ridiculous," said Kate.
Norms, Paul, Cathy and Matt were unavailable for comment as they were in the pub gloating over their names appearing in an earlier publication.

Q4 Give three benefits of using DTP.

It is a wonderful world — except for luncheon meat...

What's strange is that I can sit writing about desktop publishing, on my desktop publisher. It's a bit like one of those pictures of a bloke drawing a picture of a bloke drawing a picture of a bloke drawing a picture... Yep, the world of desktop publishing can be a wonderful spiral of fascination.

DTP and Other Presentation Software

Q1 Briefly explain these things you can do with frames in DTP software:

a) Linking

b) Wrapping

c) Layering

Q2 Write TRUE or FALSE for each of these statements:

a) Column guides or guidelines make the page look messy.

b) Column guides appear on the screen, but not on the printed document.

c) Frames can be linked across different pages of a document.

d) DTP is the most interesting subject in the world.

e) Layering can be done with text frames.

f) Queen Victoria liked garlic with her salad, but not too much. To get it just right she used to get the chef to eat the garlic and then breathe on the lettuce.

Q3 *Style sheets are templates that can save you a lot of time if you know how to use them.*

a) Briefly explain what templates and style sheets are.

b) Suggest an example where a style sheet or template would be useful.

c) Draw out a rough plan for the template suggested in part b).
You should label the different text boxes/frames and explain how they are used.

Q4 a) Briefly explain how presentations were done in the past (before specialist presentation software).

b) Give three disadvantages of this method of presentation.

Q5 *Below are statements about presentation software. Some are true and some are false.*

It produces professional-looking presentations

Presentations can only be used once

It's easy to edit and adapt presentations

Hardware, e.g. LCD projector, can be expensive.

Use of multimedia can make it difficult to get people's attention

It is easy to get carried away by the technology and produce badly-designed slides

a) Draw two columns labelled 'Advantages of presentation software' and 'Disadvantages of presentation software'. Write the true statements in the correct column.

b) Rewrite the false statements to make them true, and put them in the correct column.

Spreadsheets — The Basics

Q1 Say which of the following statements are true and which are false:

a) Spreadsheets can display numbers but not text.
b) Spreadsheets can be used to record data.
c) They can search for particular items of data.
d) They can predict when the world's going to end.
e) They can perform calculations on the data they contain.
f) They cannot produce graphs and charts.

Q2 Answer **yes** or **no** for each of the following things, to say whether a spreadsheet would be capable of doing them or not:

a) storing patients' records in a doctor's surgery
b) creating a graph to illustrate the comparative prices of CDs now and twenty years ago
c) recording the progress of a team of highly-skilled workers, all striving to attain optimum productivity levels between naps
d) calculating the amount of money saved on pizza once uncle Umberto moved back to Sicily
e) hugging my mum

Q3 Spreadsheets are made up of rows and columns. What are the individual units within them called?

Q4 a) What three things may be entered into a cell?

b) Can a cell contain more than one of these at any one time?

c) Say which of the following cells have a numerical value of zero. Rewrite the ones that do, so that they have the right numerical value.

i) -56km ii) £27.00 iii) 42.59003 iv) 100g

Q5 What is meant by the term **text string**?

What? The world's going to end? — Cool, no GCSEs then...

It's amazing how useful spreadsheets are, really. I never think about it (and I REALLY mean that), but... just imagine what it'd have been like working in a bank before spreadsheets came along. Scary.

Spreadsheets — Creating and Improving

Q1 Name the parts of the following spreadsheet, labelled **a** to **e**, using the words in the box.

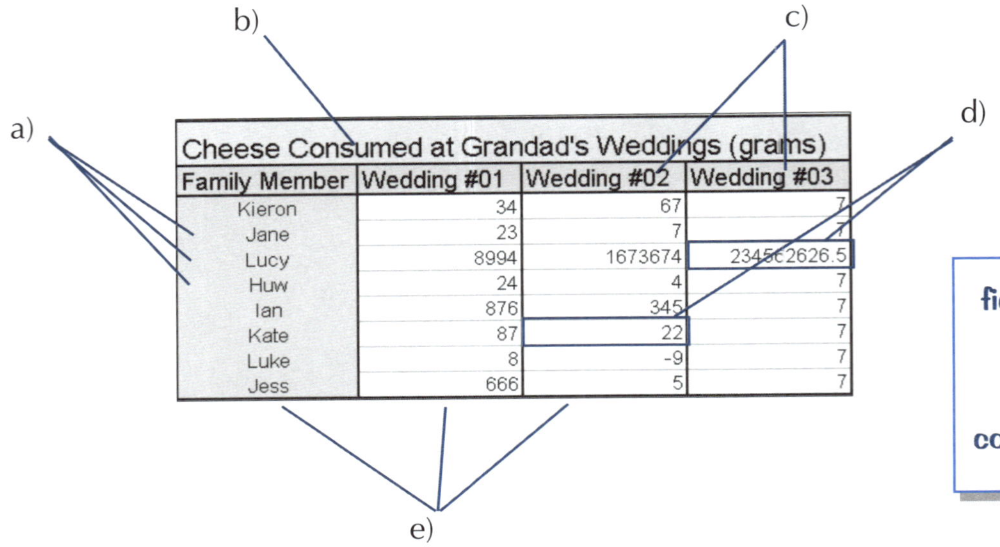

Cheese Consumed at Grandad's Weddings (grams)			
Family Member	Wedding #01	Wedding #02	Wedding #03
Kieron	34	67	7
Jane	23	7	7
Lucy	8994	1673674	2345e2626.5
Huw	24	4	7
Ian	876	345	7
Kate	87	22	7
Luke	8	-9	7
Jess	666	5	7

field names
rows
title
columns
cells

Q2 Write a sentence explaining what a **data validation formula** is.

Q3 a) Name five things you can do to the text in a spreadsheet to improve its appearance.

b) What is **conditional formatting**?

Q4 *Adrian owns his own record label. He wants to use a spreadsheet to find out which of his CDs sold the most copies last month. He needs to import all the sales figures for* Sink and Stove Records *into a spreadsheet. He imports the figures as a CSV file.*

a) What does CSV stand for?

b) Why can CSV data be easily transferred between spreadsheets, tables and databases? (In other words, what **happens** to data when you save it as a CSV file?)

c) Integrated software suites combine spreadsheets and word processors. How can you transfer data between these applications?

Conditional formatting — but only if you ask me nicely...

I reckon the best way to learn about spreadsheets is to just make yourself one and play about with it. Learning about it in theory never works — if you can't see why you'd want to do something, you'll never remember how to. You know it makes sense...

Spreadsheets — Simple Formulas

Q1 *Jim wants to write a formula that will work out how many pets each of his friends has. You can see the spreadsheet he's done below, but he's forgotten how to make it calculate the total for him. Answer the questions that follow, to help him sort his life out.*

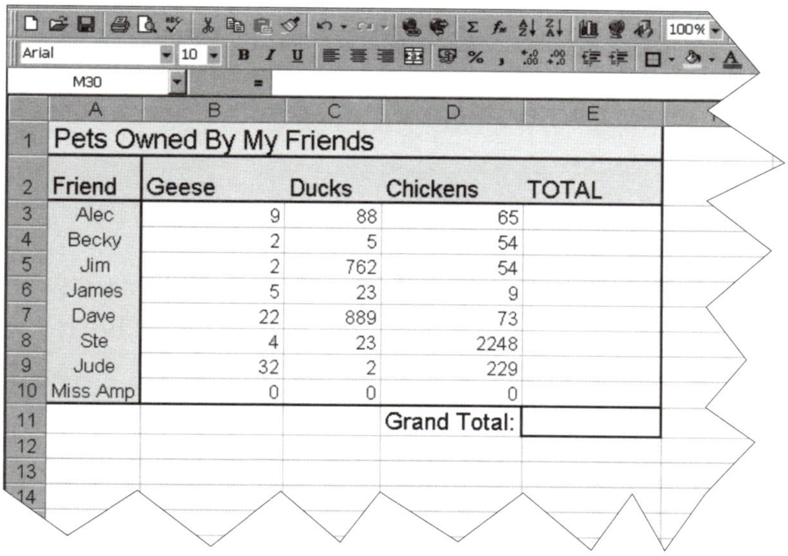

	A	B	C	D	E
1	Pets Owned By My Friends				
2	Friend	Geese	Ducks	Chickens	TOTAL
3	Alec	9	88	65	
4	Becky	2	5	54	
5	Jim	2	762	54	
6	James	5	23	9	
7	Dave	22	889	73	
8	Ste	4	23	2248	
9	Jude	32	2	229	
10	Miss Amp	0	0	0	
11				Grand Total:	
12					
13					
14					

a) Jim's clicked in cell E3. What formula should he type to find out the total number of pets that Alec has?

b) What's the quickest way he can get the rest of the cells in the TOTAL column to calculate the total of their row?

c) He also wants to know the total number of pets owned by **all** his friends. What formula should he type and which cell should it go in?

d) Does the formula in E3 have an **absolute** or **relative** cell reference?

e) What is the difference between an absolute and a relative cell reference?

f) How would you rewrite B5 as an absolute cell reference?

Q2 *Jim wants to add a column to his spreadsheet that uses the grand total to work out what percentage of the animals each of his friends owns. I don't know why. Answer the question below:*

What formula will he need to calculate Alec's percentage?

I DON'T fancy her — I was just "chicken" her out...

I think I'll write something about chickens here. And why not? It's a bit of light relief. OK, back to it — formulas. Formulas make the world go round. They're the bees' knees, so learn 'em real good.

Spreadsheets — The Trickier Stuff

Q1 Which one of the following sentences describes what logic functions do?

a) Logic functions are used to redefine values for selected cells.
b) Logic functions are used to calculate new figures.
c) Logic functions are used to tell spreadsheets how to calculate a formula.
d) Logic functions are used to produce different outputs, depending on whether certain conditions related to other cells are met.
e) Logic functions show me the money.

Q2 Write **yes** where the following things are examples of logic function outputs and **no** where they aren't.

a) where the number in a cell gives a temperature, the output could be "cold" for negative numbers and "warm" for positive numbers.
b) where people's first names are listed, the output could be their surnames.
c) where people's ages are listed, the output could be "young" for ages under 18 and "old" for ages over 80.
d) where prices of different sorts of seafood are listed, the output could be "pricey" or "cheap as skates".
e) where people you fancy are rated on a scale of one to ten, the output could be "no way" for those rated at 4 or less, "maybe" for those between 5 and 8, and "whoa momma" for those rated 9 and 10.

Q3 a) Which of the following is most likely to be the correct formula for D1 (assuming it's a logic function)?

	A	B	C	D
1	Rob	De Niro	£187,000	yes
2	Bruce	Forsyth	£6,000	no

i) =IF(C1>£100,000,"no","yes")
ii) =IF(C2>£100,000,"no","yes")
iii) =IF(C2>£100,000,"yes","no")
iv) =IF(C1>£100,000,"yes","no")

b) What would be the formula for D2 if you wanted "no" to show earnings of less than £10,000, and "yes" to show otherwise?

Q4 Explain what a **look-up table** does that a normal database doesn't do.

Q5 Explain why a large supermarket or another big retailer might use a look-up table to keep track of its products.

I wish my brain had a few of those logic functions...

Eeeek... they weren't joking when they said "tricky stuff" were they... OK, so this stuff isn't easy, but this is ICT after all — not Muppet Studies. Anyway, just think how satisfying it'll be to know all this stuff inside out. No? Oh. OK, suppose you're right. Ah well... I tried.

Spreadsheets — Graphs and Charts

Q1 Listed below are the various steps needed to produce a graph or a chart using a modern spreadsheet. Put them into the correct order. (There's a fake step too — can you guess which one?)

a) Decide whether the chart needs a key.

b) Choose a meaningful title for the chart and label any axes.

c) Highlight the data you want to use.

d) Get all the data you want to put into the graph into a single block (e.g. a column).

e) Find out what a quacksalver is.

f) Select the type of chart you want.

Q2 What is another word for a key to a chart (used by most spreadsheets)?

Q3 Name the following types of graph:

a) 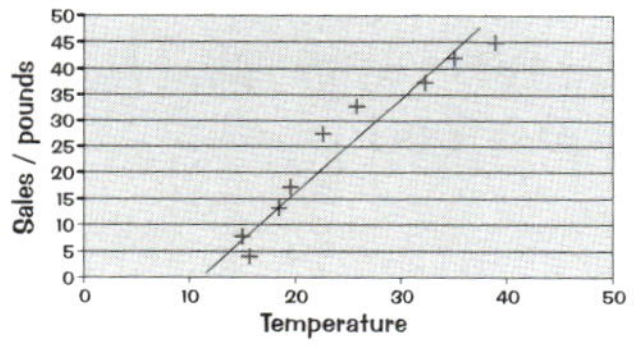

b) 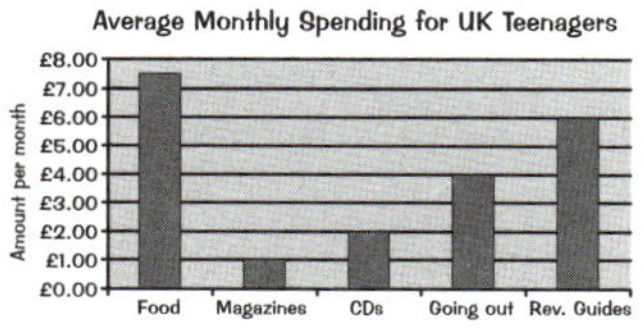

c) 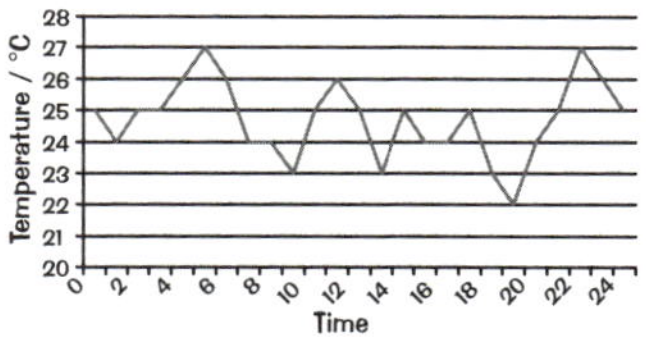

d) 

Q4 Say what each type of graph in Q3 is used for.
Use the words listed below (one for each part) to help you.

discrete categories contributions relationship not in categories

Graphs and Charts — it doesn't get any better than this...

I'm sure you'll agree by now that spreadsheets are pretty much the best thing ever. Well apart from dogs, Friends, ice cream, really small mp3 players, facial hair, pesto and Enrique Iglesias, obviously.

Databases — Creating One

Q1 The diagram below shows a database made by my mate Nick. Look at it then say whether the following statements are true or false.

People Who Owe Me Money				
First Name	**Last Name**	**Amount Owed**	**Date Borrowed**	**Relation to Me**
Kieron	Ronron	£24.50	09/09/02	nephew
Jane	Ellis	£13.76	09/09/02	butcher
Lucy	Inthesky	£0.04	08/05/01	baker
Huw	Pew	£90.09	17/04/98	candlestick maker
Ian	Tomato	£8.00	25/12/63	potato man
Kate	Winsletty	£587.65	10/10/01	neighbour
Luke	Skywalker	£99.99	17/07/95	priest
Jess	Rabbit	£90,270	06/03/01	burglar

a) Each column is a different field.

b) The "Amount Owed" column is a record.

c) "Huw" is a field.

d) The row starting with "Jess" is a record.

e) The "Date Borrowed" column is a key field.

Q2 What is a key field?

Q3 What is the main advantage of searching for data in a database instead of on paper?

Q4 Nick is making another database. He's decided what fields he wants, and has given them names. What 3 other things does each field now need?

Q5 Give an example of each of the following common data types:

a) text

b) integers

c) real numbers

d) dates

Q6 What is meant by the term **coding**, and why might you do this?

Q7 Write a paragraph explaining the difference between **flat-file** databases and **relational** databases.

Hint — think about how the data is stored, and about what a DBMS is.

Databases and spreadsheets — urge... to kill... rising...

Enough of that mean talk about ICT. I've decided that ICT is good for the heart and good for the soul. It teaches you to be strong. Strong like bull. And healthy and happy. Hoorah. Just imagine how terrible we'd all feel without ICT. There'd be no playing on computers for starters...

Databases — Sorts and Queries

Q1 What is a simple query?

Q2 *Shelley has entered the following data into her database of people who recently received compensation from a fast-food chain after finding human body-parts in their burgers.*

First Name	Last Name	City of Birth	Value	Part
Jane	Clinton	Chelsea	£25	finger
Belinda	Dobson	Carlisle	£6	toe
Irving	Jones	Berlin	£89	hairs
Eric	Walker	Morecambe	£5	toe
Bob	Beckham	Brooklyn	£26	finger
Burt	Miller	Lancaster	£6	eyelid
Tony	Stevens	Blackburn	£11	tongue
Denzel	Evans	Washington	£900	ear
Barbara	Fish	Windsor	£22	tooth
Felicity	Smith	Kendal	£87,000	toenail

She needs to sort the data in different ways. Say which person the following searches will result in:

a) Value = £26
b) Last name = S* AND City = B*
c) Value >= £1000
d) First Name = "B*" AND Part = finger
e) Part = toe AND NOT City = "Carlisle"

Q3 a) What is the name given to searches that use an asterisk in place of specific information?

b) When are these searches useful?

Q4 What is the name given to "AND", "OR" and "NOT" when used in expressions which can only be either true or false?

I think I am >= the most bored person in the world...

MAN, how do you guys cope with this stuff? There's just NO WAY that I'd stay awake. This stuff is so boring, I'm typing with one hand as I had to gnaw the other one off just to keep myself conscious. Still, it's better than being lost in space. With no monkey. THAT'd be bad. ICT is cool by comparison.

Databases — Reports

Q1 Briefly explain what a database **report** is.

Q2 The two different display formats used for reports are labelled **a** and **b**. Say what each one is called and explain why the different formats are better suited for different things.

a)

Twenty-First Century Flicks
Overdue DVD Reminder Slip

Name | **Account Number**

Tim Crewes 823006

Film Title | **Amount Overdue**

Mission Unwatchable
Mission Unwatchable 2
Top Gurn

£47.50

b)

First	Last	Account	Film 1	Film 2	Film 3	Due
Tim	Crewes	823006	Mission Unwatchable	Mission Unwatchable 2	Top Gurn	£47.50
Nicola	Kidnan	823009	Moulinex Rouge	Far and Away and Over the Hill	Dead Clam	£13.00

Q3 Why might you want to export data into a word processor or desktop publishing package?

Q4 Explain how Twenty-First Century Flicks could produce personalised letters promoting the latest Tom Crewes film for customers who liked his films.

Q5 For each of the following, say whether it is a **pro** or a **con** of using databases:

a) Searching for specific data is quicker and easier than using paper records.
b) Much less storage space is required than with a paper system.
c) Users need to be trained in how to use them properly.
d) It's easier to perform calculations with a database.
e) Large databases require expensive computer hardware and software.
f) The whole idea of a database is excessively tedious and mind-numbingly dull.

Q6 Say which of the following are good examples of a database report:

a) weekly sales figures for a magazine publisher
b) names of my crazy aunt's cats
c) number of cats owned by my crazy aunt (she owns 6)
d) number of cats visiting a vet's surgery over the past year
e) number of tins of cat food sold by a supermarket in the past six months

Database Boy isn't cool — he wears pants on the OUTside...

Man this stuff is dull. Really dull. But it's only 6 questions. Once you've done them, you could go and have a cup of tea and some cake. Mmmmmmm, cake...

Measurement — Data Logging

Q1 Which type of input device would you use in a data logging system?

Q2 Which of the following data capture requirements are suited to data logging?

a) Statistics have to be gathered from several reports.
b) Questions have to be asked of individual people.
c) Large amounts of data have to be collected.
d) The data has to be collected over a very long period of time.
e) Written information has to be transferred to a computer system.
f) Data has to be collected every 1/10 of a second.
g) Temperature has to be monitored inside a large deep-freeze.

Q3 Name the two types of signal produced by data logging input sensors.

Q4 Copy and complete the table below to suggest a use for each type of sensor and classify each sensor as analogue or digital.

Sensor Measures	Use of Sensor	Digital/Analogue
Pressure	Counting cars approaching a set of traffic lights.	Digital
Light		
Radioactivity		
Sound		
Infra-red		
Air pressure		

Q5 a) Many of the sensors used in data logging systems produce analogue signals. What must be done to an analogue signal before it can be used by a computer, and what equipment is used to do this?

b) CSV files are often used to store data collected by a data logging system. Explain what CSV stands for and explain why a CSV file might be used.

Logging Period and Logging Interval

Q1 Copy and complete the following definitions:

The logging period is...
The logging interval is...

Q2 What formula would you use to determine the number of readings taken during a logging period?

Q3 Copy out the following sentences, using the word bank below to fill in the blanks.

The .... period of a system is determined by the .... of time it takes the process being monitored to be .... The logging .... is usually determined by the length of the logging period. The shorter the process being monitored, the .... the logging interval. Monitoring the growth of plants will require a logging .... of weeks with .... logging intervals. Monitoring the progress of a chemical reaction that completes in a matter of seconds would require a logging period of less than a .... with a logging interval of 1/10 of a second or less.

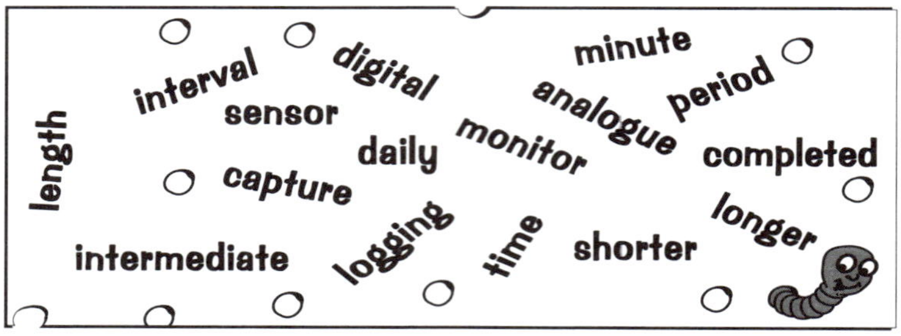

Q4 Copy and complete the table of data capture requirements below to indicate where data logging would be used and why.

Data capture requirement	Suitable for data logging	Reason
• A questionnaire to discover how many people in one street recycle glass.	Yes/No	....
• The number of cars using a busy road over a period of 1 week.	Yes/No	....
• An opinion poll on the popularity of the government.	Yes/No	....
• The acceleration of an athlete in the first second of a 100 m race.	Yes/No	....
• The temperature in the crater of an active volcano.	Yes/No	....

Q5 List four advantages of using data logging equipment.

Control — Basic Systems

Q1 What are the two main types of control systems?

Q2 Complete the following sentence by selecting one of the phrases from the list below:

Dedicated control systems...

a) carry out a pre-programmed set of instructions.

b) use a computer to process the data from sensors.

c) do not use sensors.

d) require human intervention to control their output devices.

Q3 Draw a block diagram of a typical computer control system with a feedback loop.

Q4 a) Control systems are often required to drive analogue devices (like electric motors or electric lights) by varying the current to the output device. What type of interface does the computer need to communicate with these types of device?

b) Many of the sensors used in a control system are also analogue. What type of interface does the computer need to process the data provided by analogue sensors?

Q5 a) Draw a diagram of a computer control system that controls the floodlights of a sports ground, depending on how much light there is. Use the components below.

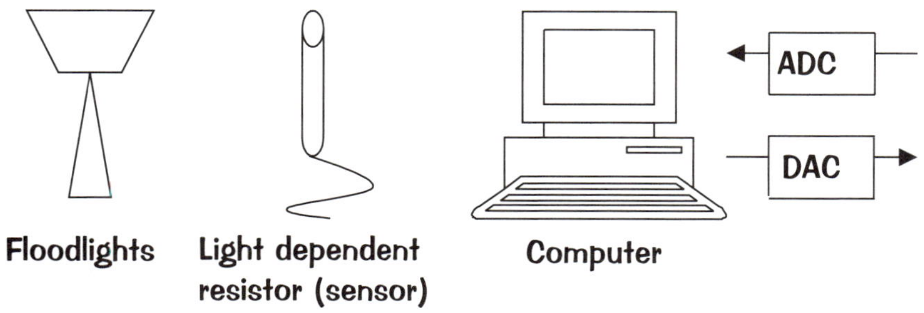

b) Describe what part each of these components plays in the control system.

c) Why would it be inadvisable to place the light sensors below the floodlights?

Control Systems — Two Examples

Q1 What are the two ways of developing instructions to operate commercial robots?

a) show and tell
b) do it once and remember
c) inbuilt control
d) teach and learn
e) feedback loop

Q2 Which of the ways to develop instructions, from Q1 above, is described below?

> A set of instructions is written and the robot is programmed with them. The writers of the instructions observe the robot in operation. The writers of the instructions then modify the instructions to rectify any errors or improve the way the robot performs the task.

Q3 Car manufacturers often use robots to perform simple tasks on their assembly line. List the advantages and disadvantages of using robots in manufacturing.

Q4 Suggest the sensors that might be used by a robot to detect obstructions and avoid safety hazards when people are working in the same area.

Q5 a) A computer control system is used to control the temperature in a greenhouse. It automatically opens the windows as the temperature rises and closes them as it drops. With the aid of a diagram explain how the computer, a temperature sensor and electric motors would be used by the control system.

b) The plants in the greenhouse are fed with liquid plant nutrient. The owners of the greenhouse decide to install a dedicated control system to feed the plants three times a day. Explain how such a control system would work.

I ended up in a ditch — no sensor direction...

Control systems aren't that difficult. I understand them and I was born years ago — before control systems, before Star Wars, before JFK, before muesli...

Process Control and Control Language

Q1 Pick the names of the key elements of an industrial process control system from the collection of computer devices given below:

computer keyboard automated device mouse
monitor sensor scanner digital camera

Q2 Name the system where output data is sent back into the control system and used to make adjustments to keep the output within specified limits.

Q3 Draw and annotate a simple diagram to show a control system that regulates the supply of oil in an oil pipeline. The system should use a pressure sensor in the pipeline, and a computer to control the speed of the pump that delivers the oil to the pipeline.

Q4 Explain what each of the following LOGO commands does:

a) PENDOWN
b) PENUP
c) RIGHT X (where X is a number 1 to 360)
d) LEFT X (where X is a number 1 to 360)
e) FORWARD X (where X is any whole number)
f) BACKWARD X (where X is any whole number)
g) REPEAT X [<any of the commands above>] (where X is any whole number)

Q5 What shape would be drawn by the following LOGO program?

```
PENDOWN
FORWARD 100
RIGHT 90
FORWARD 50
REPEAT 3 [LEFT 120 FORWARD 100]
PENUP
```

Q6 What is a computer program?
What must be done so that a machine can understand the program?

Modelling and Simulation — Basic Stuff

Q1 a) What is the name for an artificial re-creation of an object that's created using programmed instructions and equations?

b) When a computer is used to mimic real life it is called:

i) a model
ii) a program
iii) a simulation
iv) hacking

Q2 From the list of words below, pick the things that are used to create a model:

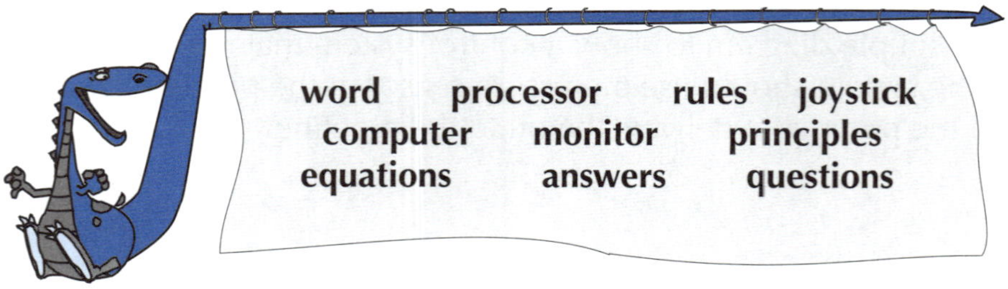

Q3 List four different types of computer model.

Q4 List three advantages and three disadvantages of using computers to model situations.

Q5 Expert systems are one type of computer model. The knowledge base, rules and questions of an expert system work together to provide the users of a system with answers to their problems. Explain how this works.

Q6 Virtual reality systems need more than just graphics to give the user of the system a sense of realism. Explain how sound and physical output devices (like rumble devices in games pads) are used to enhance the virtual reality experience.

Hurl malice at yourself — a spite simulation...

Models and simulations are different. A model is just a simplified description of something to help with calculations / predictions. A simulation is more specific — it's when a computer is pretending to be something else (usually by following a mathematical model). So there.

Spreadsheet Models and Simulations

Q1 Which of the following are used by spreadsheets to describe the rules of a model?

a) descriptions
b) cells
c) simulations
d) predictions
e) formulas

Q2 Copy out the following sentence, using the word bank below to fill in the blanks.

Spreadsheets use .... to create .... The formulas describe the .... of the model. By changing the .... in the spreadsheet, the model can be used to answer .... questions.

models worksheet cells rows rules formulas
address what-if column reference variables

Q3 What form of output (other than numbers) is available in a spreadsheet to make the results of a simulation easier to understand?

Q4 a) A café uses a spreadsheet to calculate the cost of the food it sells. What rule should go in cell E1 to calculate the price of hot dogs?

	A	B	C	D	E
1	Hot Dog	Sausage	Bread bun	Profit	Price
2		£0.50	£0.10	£0.50	

Hint — the price of a hot dog is the cost of the: Sausage + Bread bun + Profit

b) The café has heard the price of bread is about to rise. They want to perform a what-if analysis to find out how this will affect the price of hot dogs. What would they change in the spreadsheet to do this?

Q5 Give a definition of the term **what-if analysis**.

What-if — I woke up and ICT didn't exist...

Maybe you don't live in the twenty-first century at all. Maybe you'll wake up, clean out the cowshed, catch smallpox, eat a dodo and think, "Actually, spreadsheet models were pretty cool."

Simulations — Flight Simulators

Q1 For each of the devices below, say whether they would be used as **input** or **output** devices in a flight simulator.

a) monitor
b) joystick
c) hydraulic pistons
d) cockpit controls

Q2 Give two advantages and one disadvantage of using a flight simulator to train pilots.

Q3 Draw and label a diagram to show how the control system for a flight simulator would work, in terms of inputs and outputs to a computer.

Q4 Flight simulators have an interior that is an exact replica of a real aircraft cockpit. List three environmental conditions that can be simulated in this closed environment.

Q5 a) Flight simulators must respond to the pilot instantly. What type of data processing is this?

b) Flight simulators create a feedback loop linking the output of the flight simulator to the input from the pilot. Explain how the pilot's use of the controls is used in the feedback loop to change the behaviour of the flight simulator.

c) Draw a diagram of the feedback loop described in b) above.

Q6 There are various levels of simulation. Describe the following:

a) a flight simulator created for a computer game
b) a flight simulator created using virtual reality
c) a full flight simulator

Internet Basics

Q1 a) Which of the following statements best describes the Internet?

i) A set of web pages all linked together.
ii) A set of computers connected by high speed communication lines.
iii) A large electronic post office.
iv) The largest LAN in the world.

b) Who was the Internet originally developed by?

i) UK Universities
ii) Japanese Industry
iii) The United States Government
iv) The USSR Government
v) United States Universities

c) What task was the Internet initially developed to carry out?

Q2 All areas of IT use abbreviations, and the Internet has loads.
Say what each of the following Internet abbreviations stand for:

a) WWW b) ISP c) ISDN d) ADSL e) WAN

Q3 a) List the hardware and software that a user would need to connect to the Internet from home using a phone line.

b) Produce a simple drawing, using the items you listed in your answer to part a), to illustrate how the hardware used by a home user connects them to the Internet via an ISP.

Q4 *The Internet can be broken down into several services. The most commonly used of these services are e-mail and the World Wide Web.*

Write a paragraph to explain what the World Wide Web is.

Q5 a) What are the differences between the older, slower ways of connecting to the Internet and the newer, faster ways?

b) How have faster connections changed what we use the Internet for?

E-mail

Q1 Which e-mail feature saves e-mail addresses, allowing you to retrieve the address without retyping it?

Q2 Home computers are one way of sending e-mail. List **two** other ways of e-mailing from home.

Q3 Give **two** precautions you can take to prevent your PC from contracting a virus from e-mails.

Q4 Which e-mail feature would you use to send a sound or video file with your e-mail?

Q5 With the aid of a diagram show how e-mail is transferred between an e-mail program, an ISP and the Internet. Remember to include both the mail client's In/Out boxes and the ISP's mailbox.

Q6 Write a sentence about each of the advantages and disadvantages of using e-mail shown in the table below.

Advantages	Disadvantages
SPEED	ACCESS
COST	VIRUSES
EASE	

Q7 Copy and complete this paragraph about web-based e-mail. Fill in the gaps using words in the box below.

Web-based e-mail does not use a local e-mail client to .... and forward .... Users of web-based e-mail read and compose new e-mail via a .... The e-mails are retrieved .... from and transmitted directly to the users' inboxes and outboxes on the ISP server. As web-based e-mail does not use a .... on a client PC, e-mail can be read and written from .... PC.

web browser	*any*	*directly*
store	*local store*	*e-mail*

Using the World Wide Web — Navigating

Q1 The address of a web page on the World Wide Web is specified by its URL. What do the initials URL stand for?

a) Universal Resource Locator
b) Uniform Resource Link
c) Uniform Resource Locator
d) Unique Resource Link
e) Unique Resource Locator

Q2 For each of the following, say whether it is a web browser, type of omelette or neither.

a) Firefish
b) Cheese and mushroom
c) Opera
d) Spanish
e) Goats cheese and pea
f) Netscape
g) Salmon and Asparagus
h) Firefox
i) Plain
j) Ballet
k) Internet Explorer
l) No Escape

Q3 *A URL is made up of several parts. These parts allow a web browser to find the specific web page given in the URL. Some names for parts of URLs are listed below:*

protocol	domain name	domain type
country code	path	HTML filename

Copy the following URL and use the parts listed above to label it:

<http://www.cgpbooks.co.uk/ICT/default.htm>

Q4 *Browsing the web is good fun, but not the most efficient way to find information. A better way to find information on the Internet is through a search engine or a portal.*

a) How do search engines help you to find information on the Internet?

b) How do portals help you find information on the Internet?

Q5 *Searches can help you find information on the Internet or within a particular website, but often a simple search will not bring up exactly what you were looking for. Advanced searches using logical operators can be used to change the matches returned.*

Explain how these search operators can be used to change the matches returned:

a) AND b) OR c) NOT

Navigating and Downloading

Q1 a) What is a hyperlink?

b) What makes a hyperlink stand out from the normal text on a web page?

c) How can a web browser show you that you have already followed a text hyperlink?

Q2 Following hyperlinks and typing in the URL of a web page are two of the methods used by web browsers to navigate the World Wide Web. List **three** other features of a web browser that help users quickly navigate the web and locate their favourite web pages.

Q3 Hyperlinks can take you to other websites. Name **two** other 'places' hyperlinks can take you to.

Q4 Many web browsers provide users with a 'History' feature. Write a short paragraph to describe what a web browser 'History' feature does.

Q5 *Large web pages can be time-consuming to download. To speed up the download of files and web pages, designers of web sites often compress their files.*

a) Write a paragraph to explain what file compression is and why it speeds up the download of web pages.

b) The text part of a web page is quite small and rarely needs to be compressed. Create a list of the type of information that can be included in a web page and that would benefit from compression.

Q6 Web browsers also use various techniques to speed up the display of web pages. The most common of these techniques is the use of a 'cache'. Write a paragraph to explain what a cache is and how it speeds up the display of web pages.

Q7 *Below is a taskbar of an Internet browser.*

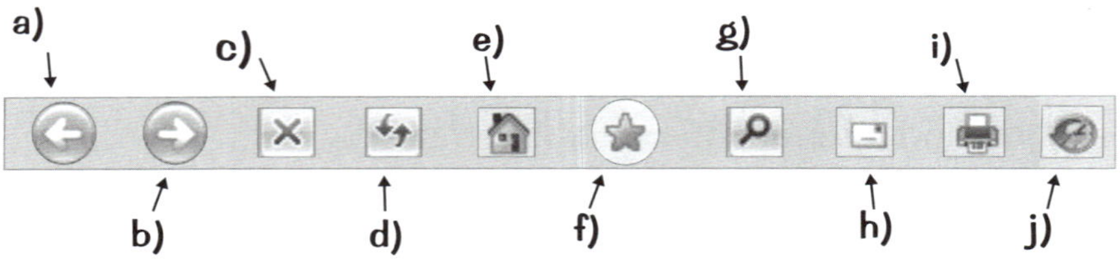

a) For each label a) to j), match the part shown to the following functions:

i) Stop ii) Search iii) Email iv) Back v) Refresh

vi) Favourites vii) History viii) Forward ix) Home x) Print

b) Write a sentence about the function of each part of the taskbar.

Web Page Design

Q1 Web pages are written using HTML. What do the initials HTML stand for?

Q2 HTML documents are text files, but like all programming languages HTML has a strict syntax (otherwise it won't work). List **three types** of software that support the saving of files in HTML format.

Q3 Name another programming language that you might use to give your web page some interactive content.

Q4 Look at the web page on the right and use your knowledge of web page design to comment on the following features:

a) Clarity of appearance.
b) Relevance of information for visitors (both first-time and regular users).
c) The use of text.
d) Attractiveness of appearance.

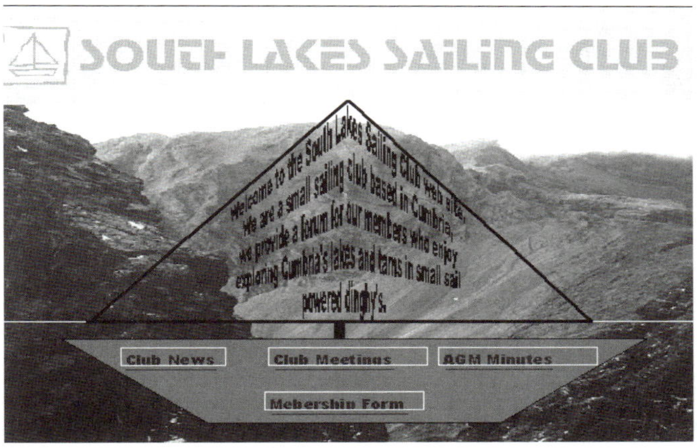

Q5 Explain the following types of web page content, giving examples of each.

a) Dynamic
b) Interactive

www.nastynastyspiders.com — a great webby page...

Web pages should look good, but much more important is that they're easy to use, and they load quickly. Because otherwise the user will get really annoyed with it, and never come back. Ever. Like those pages with millions of animations and sounds everywhere that only appear after an hour.

Using the Internet — Data Security

Q1 Why might using the Internet to transmit private, sensitive information be a problem?

Q2 *To maintain the privacy of sensitive information some websites encrypt data. To read the information it has to be decrypted.*

a) Use the information given below to decrypt the following message.

Each letter in the message has been replaced by a letter four places further on in the alphabet — i.e. "a" is replaced by "e", "b" is replaced by "f", etc.

w, x, y, z are cyclic so: "w" becomes "a", "x" becomes "b", "y" becomes "c", "z" becomes "d".

The message is: *xli oic mw mr xli higvctxmsr sj xlmw qiwweki*

Obviously encryption techniques used on the Internet are much more complicated than this.

b) What name do you give to the information outlined in a) above that explained what had been done to encrypt the message?

Q3 Use **one** sentence to answer each of the following two questions:

a) What is a virus?

b) What is a secure site?

Q4 Organisations need to protect their computer systems from hackers and viruses.

a) What does the word hacking mean?

b) List **three steps** that an organisation might take to protect its systems from hackers.

Q5 On-line shopping is growing in popularity. Describe how on-line shopping sites use electronic 'shopping baskets' and credit card information to allow people to buy stuff.

Q6 *The Internet has become such a popular method of sharing information that many companies use the Internet model to distribute information to their employees on a company 'intranet'.*

Give an example of where an intranet could be used and describe how an organisation can prevent unauthorised access to their intranet.

Viruses aren't all bad — you might get days off school...

So that's web security. Are you relieved? I know I am. I like checking my e-mail and seeing what my mates have been up to on holiday, but all this data security nonsense is doing my head in.

User-Generated Content

Q1 Give **three** ways that Internet users can share knowledge, opinions or experiences.

Q2 What is meant by the term "hive mind"?

Q3 Give **two** examples of websites that might use the hive mind effect

Q4 Copy and complete the table using the phrases given to show the advantages and disadvantages of Online Communities.

Advantages	Disadvantages
1.	1.
2.	2.
3.	3.

i) Regular contributors can be given special privileges and roles within a community.
ii) It's possible that you can end up spending more time online than in the real world.
iii) Privileges can be abused and can ruin the community for other users.
iv) There's not an easy way to check that people are who they say they are.
v) A community of contributors can produce lots of accurate and useful information.
vi) People enjoy interacting with each other and having a sense of community.

Q5 *Blogs are a popular type of User-Generated Content.*
Explain what a blog is and give an example of what it might be used for.

Kelly had a blogged sink.

User-Generated Content

Q1 Copy and complete the following paragraph using the words provided on the computer screen.

Lots of people .... content to websites on a regular basis. It's quite difficult to keep track of .... is being added, and .... adding it. Most user-generated content can't be .... — there are no specific .... to follow to make sure content is .... Most websites rely on other .... to edit their content. And of course, some information is just rubbish — just because it's on a .... website doesn't always mean it's reliable.

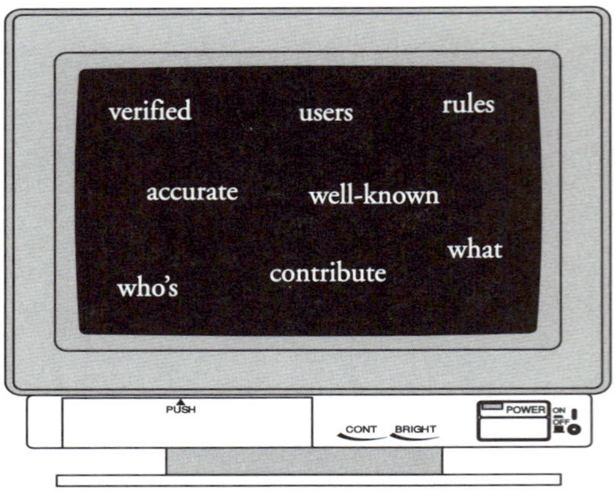

Q2 Define the following legal issues and say how they might be a problem for websites that are based around User-Generated Content:

a) Copyright
b) Libel

Q3 Why don't some websites monitor User-Generated Content?

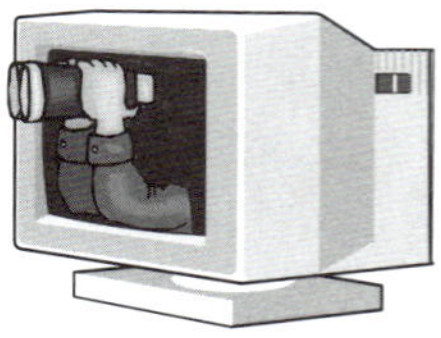

He monitored. Like he'd never monitored before.

Q4 What methods can be used to monitor content?

Q5 *Some sites attempt to moderate user-generated content.*

Find the true statements below and summarise why it might be difficult to apply the law:

1) Monitoring means that the hosts are too busy to feed their cats.
2) Monitoring shows that the hosts are taking steps to prevent copyright and libel occurring.
3) The hosts don't have a responsibility to review uploaded content.
4) Hosting a website means that you're not allowed to host dinner parties anymore.
5) If a website is monitored or controlled, it means that the hosts become responsible for the content of the web pages.

Social Networking

Q1 What is a thread (in relation to a discussion board)?

Q2 How do websites with message boards try to protect themselves against unwanted posts?

Q3 What is spam? Describe the different forms it might take.

Q4 Describe how trolling affects message boards.

Q5 Pick the correct words to complete the following sentences:

1) People having conversations via a messaging service receive messages eventually / immediately.
2) To chat, both users have to be connected to the Internet / sitting on a bench.
3) Instant Messaging is more personal / formal than emails and less exciting / intrusive than a phone call.
4) You can talk face to face if both users have a webcam / face.

Q6 How have Instant Messaging providers responded to the concern that chatrooms and chatting services might not be safe for children?

Trolling can make everyone feel a bit orc-ward...

The chances are you're fairly familiar with instant messaging and all the stuff that goes with it. But make sure you can answer these questions — just 'cos you use it don't mean you know it...

Social Networking

Q1 Social networking websites combine lots of interactive features — list **five** things you could use such a website for.

Q2 Give **four** pieces of information you could include on your profile page.

Q3 Give **three** examples of information it wouldn't be sensible to include.

Q4 Give three personal details you could search by to find someone on a social network website.

Q5 Before they can be linked over a social website, what do both users have to do?

a) A little dance.
b) Make some home-made cheese.
c) Confirm they know each other.
d) Make sure they look presentable.

Social Networking websites mean you don't have to sit there staring at people that you hate anymore.

Q6 Give **two** advantages and **two** disadvantages of social networks.

Online Audio and Video

Q1 Do professional companies or amateur users provide most of the internet's video and audio content?

Q2 Give some examples of the following as provided by professional companies:

a) Audio content

b) Video content

Q3 Are the following devices suitable for amateurs who want to record videos to upload:

1) Mobile phone
2) A pillow
3) A webcam
4) An overhead projector
5) Plasticine
6) A digital camera
7) A recording studio

Q4 Describe citizen journalism in your own words.

Luke's vlog was less than attention grabbing.

Q5 What is a vlog?

Q6 Briefly outline the copyright problems associated with online audio and video.

If you don't copyright, you'll make loads of mistakes...

The security issues around content and sensitive information (stuff about people) are really important to these pages. Sure, websites are fun — but there are pretty grey areas around their control.

Online Software

Q1 What is the main aim of online software?

Q2 Describe how online software can allow many users to have input into the creation of documents.

No-one really knew what they were getting so hung up about.

Q3 What were the early capabilities of online software?

Q4 How is online software developing?

Q5 Copy and complete the following paragraph to highlight the problems with online software:

The .... of online software isn't quite as .... as you might be used to on your own computer. Compared to loading documents direct from your .... , it can sometimes .... to access them online. There can be problems .... and .... files if they're saved online, and sometimes files don't .... properly and can become .... There are also some .... restrictions on online files as well as the general .... issues with saving something on the Internet.

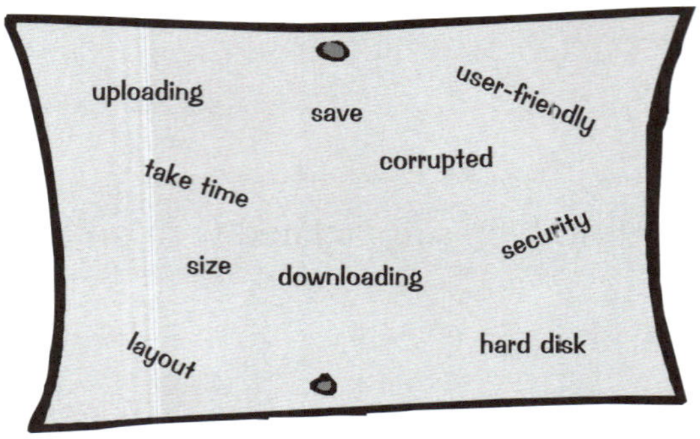

I used online software on my bike...it kept crashing.

Not seriously. Only into trees and stuff. Maybe the odd squirrel. But there you have it — the Internet in a nutshell for you in section 8. I didn't say it was a small nutshell, but it's worth learning.

Computers in Shops

Q1 What do the initials EPOS stand for?

Q2 What do the initials EFTPOS stand for?

Q3 *Bar codes usually end with a check digit.*

a) What is a check digit?

b) Why are check digits used in bar codes?

Q4 *The diagram below represents a supermarket EPOS system. The arrows connecting the components of the system represent the information that is transferred around the system.*

a) What information is passed along arrow 1 from the laser scanner to the supermarket's computer system?

b) What information is passed along arrow 2 from the computer to the till?

c) What information would you expect to be stored in the supermarket's database? (Include three things)

Q5 Describe how EPOS systems control the level of stock in a supermarket.

Q6 How do shops try to reduce the risk of credit card fraud?

Computers in Banks

Q1 List three ways that banks use ICT.

Q2 *Banks use magnetic ink to write information on cheques.*

a) What do the initials MICR stand for?

b) What information is printed on a cheque in magnetic ink?

c) Why is magnetic ink used on a cheque?

Q3 Below is the start of a data flow diagram that describes how a cheque is processed. Complete the diagram. Include steps to show what the payee's bank, the clearing house and the customer's bank do with the cheque.

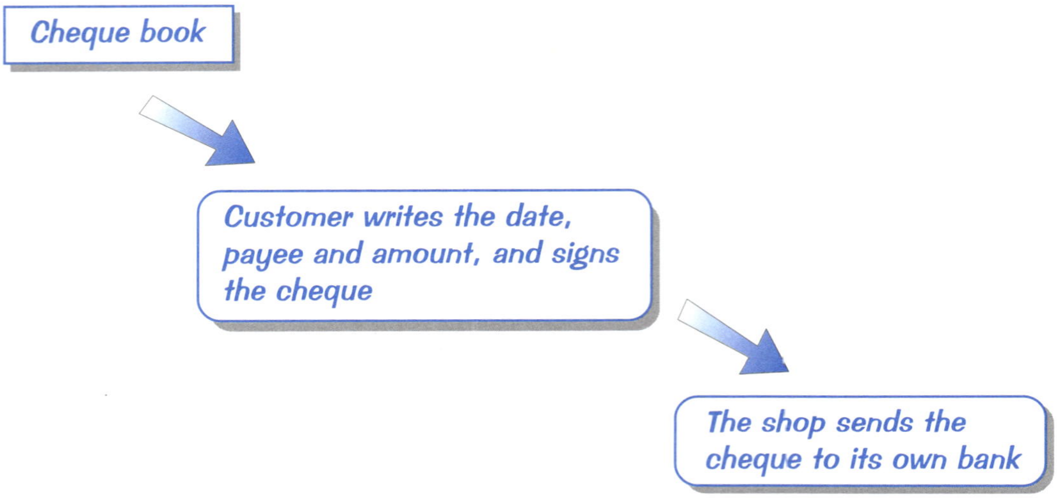
Cheque book
Customer writes the date, payee and amount, and signs the cheque
The shop sends the cheque to its own bank

Q4 What information would you expect to find on the magnetic strip of a credit or debit card?

Q5 When the user of an ATM types in their PIN number, the PIN is checked to ensure that the person using the card is the owner. What type of check is this?

Q6 Home banking is becoming more popular with the growth of home computers. What hardware and software would the user of a home computer need to use a home banking system?

Q7 Give two advantages and two disadvantages of home banking, from the bank's point of view.

The Electronic Office

Q1 A paperless office is one where computers are used to communicate information, instead of printed documents. Answer the following questions:

a) List three types of IT technology you would expect to be used in a paperless office.

b) What do the initials EDI stand for?

c) What is an intranet?

d) Why is e-mail an essential part of a paperless office?

Q2 List the advantages and the disadvantages of a paperless office.

Q3 *Last year the Pit of Boredom ICT company and its sister organisation, the Big Hole of Hell Workbook company, sent information to each other by post. This year they decided to modernise and send stuff electronically.*

Explain how EDI could be used by the two companies to exchange information.

Q4 Describe the hardware and software required to provide videoconferencing facilities in an office.

Q5 Describe the benefits offered to an office by the introduction of videoconferencing.

They seek it here, they seek it there...

They seek it flippin' everywhere. Is it in heaven? Is it in hell? That damned elusive... electronic office...

Computers in Schools

Q1 a) What do the initials CMIS stand for?

b) Name two types of information you would expect to find in a school's CMIS.

c) Where might pupils' records be stored in a school's CMIS?

Q2 a) What do the initials OMR stand for?

b) How is OMR used to help register pupils?

c) What other computerised method could a school use to register pupils?

Q3 List two advantages and two disadvantages of a school CMIS system.

Q4 Copy and complete the sentences using the words in the box below.

Computer-aided learning uses .... to generate on-screen .... and computer-aided .... The pupil's ability is assessed and a learning programme of an appropriate .... is provided. The pupil therefore gets an .... learning programme. Another element of an electronic classroom is an interactive .... board. All the computers in the class are .... to the board, which is at the front of the classroom. It means .... can watch a .... by one pupil. The board can also .... the teacher's board notes into a .... which can be saved and used again.

software convert level presentation individualised everyone
display connected learning materials assessment computer file

Cars and Traffic Management Systems

Q1 The DVLA holds a large database of all the cars and drivers registered in the UK. List three types of data held about:

a) drivers

b) cars

Q2 Give a short description of the following two methods of controlling traffic lights:

a) fixed-time mode

b) vehicle-activated mode

Q3 What type of sensor is used in speed cameras to measure the speed of a moving vehicle?

Q4 How is information from speed cameras and from the DVLA vehicle registration database used to identify speeding drivers?

Q5 Describe how a car park management system stops cars entering a car park when it is full.

Q6 What do the initials GIS stand for?

No, I am Trafficonicus...

Think about Spartacus (the film, not reality). He was prepared to just go for it, start a revolt, march around the country, live in a tent and eat berries from trees. (This is the only way to escape the traffic management page.)

Computers in the Home

Q1 List three common uses of home computers.

Q2 What specialist hardware and software does a home computer need to access the Internet?

Q3 a) Name three types of input sensor used by burglar alarms.

b) Describe two forms of output used by burglar alarms to indicate that an intruder has been detected.

Q4 What is an embedded computer?

Q5 List four household machines that are controlled by an embedded computer.

Q6 Describe two ideas of what home computer systems might be like in the future.

Then he said — "Help me, I'm about to explode..."

What if someone said that to you? Say they had overdone the sherbet dips and were having a very nasty turn with fizzing yellow stuff inside their stomach. Would computers help you then?

Computer Applications — Other Stuff

Q1 a) What type of data does a meteorological data logging system collect?

b) Describe how a weather map can be produced using data from weather sensors.

c) How are computer models used in modern weather forecasting?

Q2 Name two advantages of virtual house visits — one for the estate agent and one for the buyer.

Q3 Copy and complete the sentences, using words from the box below:

Estate agents collect .... of a property and give prospective .... a written description of it. It's often hard for them to tell what the property is really .... and whether it's worth .... the property. One way of solving this problem is for estate agents to use .... and interactive software to produce .... of the property.

viewing dung buyers like
elephants digital cameras engines
details unloading virtual tours

Q4 How might an interior designer make use of a computer package to help their customers visualise the new designs they have in mind for their house?

And she said — "bicarbonate of soda would help"

Ah, Bicarbonate of Soda Studies — a new GCSE with a nice workbook asking questions about utterly irrelevant things, like the 'Uses of Bicarbonate of Soda in the Real World'. Let me dream...

Computers and the Law

Q1 *To legally install software on your computer you need a software licence.*

a) Where does a single-user licence allow you to install software?

b) Where would it be illegal to install software with a single-user licence?

Q2 Copy and complete the table below to show during which years the Data Protection Act, the Copyright, Design and Patents Act and the Computer Misuse Act were introduced.

Year Law Introduced	Law
1984	
1989	
1990	

Q3 What does the Copyright, Design and Patents Act make it illegal to do to a computer file?

Q4 Data subjects are the people that organisations hold information about. What does the Data Protection Act entitle data subjects to do?

Q5 List the eight principles of the Data Protection Act.

Q6 Describe how the laws in the Copyright, Design and Patents Act are often broken when:

a) software is installed.

b) using text or images found on the Internet in your own publications.

c) making copies of computer software CDs.

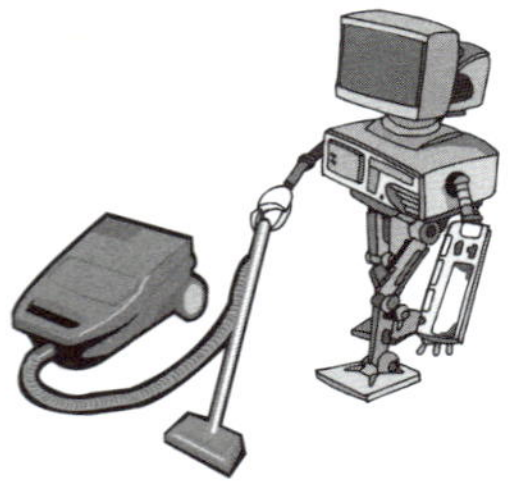

"But I'm quite clever really," sighed the computer. "Get on with the hoovering," said Ron.

Q7 *One of the purposes of the Computer Misuse Act was to help prevent the spread of computer viruses.*

State the three things the Act made illegal.

Computers and the Workplace

Q1 Computer systems and robots have replaced many repetitive jobs. Match the job to the computer hardware or software that could replace it:

Job		Computer hardware/software	
a)	secretary typing letters on a typewriter	i)	spreadsheet
b)	assembly worker spray-painting cars	ii)	database
c)	print worker typesetting text and pictures	iii)	word processor
d)	book-keeper recording petty cash in a book	iv)	robot
e)	filing clerk filing paper in a filing cabinet	v)	desktop publishing

Q2 Computer systems also create jobs. Copy and complete the table of tasks below by indicating the job title of the people doing each task.

Task	Job Title
Design computer system	
Write computer software	
Connect computers on a network	

Q3 Explain what **hot-desking** is.

Q4 What is **teleworking**?

Q5 List two advantages and two disadvantages of the increasing use of computers in the workplace.

I reckon R2D2 could do my job...

Actually that would be quite an interesting experiment. Thing is, if no-one could tell the difference I'd be free — free to leave work, go on holiday, buy a little restaurant near the beach...

Computer Use — Health and Safety Issues

Q1 Which of the following make computer-related health problems worse?

a) not using the equipment properly

b) working when you have a bad cough

c) poor design and arrangement of equipment

d) very little bears freaking you out

Q2 Describe how computers can cause the following health problems:

a) Repetitive Strain Injury (RSI)

b) headaches and eye strain

c) back problems

Q3 Name four pieces of equipment / furniture that help decrease the risks of using computers.

Q4 Describe five things the Health and Safety Act says employers need to do to maintain a healthy environment for their employees who use computers.

Q5 This picture shows a computer being used badly. Name three problems with this set-up.

Social, Moral and Ethical Issues

Q1 How are social issues different from moral and ethical issues?

Q2 Is the following sentence true or false?

All the information available on the Internet is accurate and unbiased.

Q3 List three types of information that can be found on the Internet that could be offensive to people.

Q4 *Many people think the Internet should be subject to some form of censorship.*

a) Describe one advantage of applying censorship to the Internet.

b) Describe one disadvantage of applying censorship to the Internet.

Q5 Pupils often use pictures and text from the Internet in their projects. Why might this be an ethical issue?

Q6 Describe an ethical issue raised by computers taking over some repetitive tasks in the workplace.

Q7 Give one advantage and one disadvantage of increased government surveillance of personal Internet use.

Section Ten — the smallest section in the world...

...and it's almost over.

The small but mighty Section Ten spent his early years touring Eastern Europe as part of a circus. He escaped and, after three years recovering his dignity, finally found happiness in this book.

Social, Moral and Ethical Issues

Q1 Explain what is meant by 'information rich' and 'information poor'.

Q2 The growth of e-mail means we don't spend as much time talking face to face with people. Give two negative effects that could result from this.

Q3 Copy and complete the following sentences, using words from the box below:

Some people think that parents who give their children .... are making it .... for them to become independent and .... There are also worries that increased use of the Internet and .... results in people spending less time .... There is a fear this could lower levels of .... , especially among .... people.

mobile phones **young** **pigeons**
reading **headaches** **harder** **self-reliant**
literacy **parcels** **computer games**

Q4 Give two disadvantages of the faster pace of work caused by the introduction of computers.

Q5 *Computers can be good for the environment.*

a) How might teleworking and the ability to videoconference help the environment?

b) How might the ability to view all information on-screen help the environment?

They think it's all over — it is now...

Goodbye ICT. Goodbye question boxes. Goodbye copy and complete. Goodbye tables. Goodbye boredom. See you, hate to leave you. But I'm definitely going, nevertheless...